DEAR
GIRLS

DEAR GIRLS

Intimate Tales, Untold Secrets &
Advice for Living Your Best Life

ALI WONG

RANDOM HOUSE  NEW YORK

Published in the United States by Random House,
an imprint and division of Penguin Random House LLC, New York.

RANDOM HOUSE and the HOUSE colophon are
registered trademarks of Penguin Random House LLC.

Originally published in hardcover in the United States
by Random House, an imprint and division of
Penguin Random House LLC, in 2019.

LIBRARY OF CONGRESS CATALOGING-IN-PUBLICATION DATA
Names: Wong, Ali, author.
Title: Dear girls: intimate tales, untold secrets & advice
for living your best life/ Ali Wong.
Description: First edition. | New York: Random House, 2019.
Identifiers: LCCN 2019022835 (print) | LCCN 2019022836 (ebook) |
ISBN 9780525508854 (paperback) | 9780525508847 (ebook)
Subjects: LCSH: Wong, Ali. | Comedians—United States—Biography. |
Women comedians—United States—Biography. | Television writers—
United States—Biography. | Actors—United States—Biography. |
Conduct of life—Humor. | Asian American women—Humor.
Classification: LCC PN2287.W555 A3 2019 (print) |
LCC PN2287.W555 (ebook) | DCC 792.7/6028092 [B]—dc23
LC record available at https://lccn.loc.gov/2019022835
LC ebook record available at https://lccn.loc.gov/2019022836

Printed in the United States of America on acid-free paper

randomhousebooks.com

2 4 6 8 9 7 5 3

Book design by Elizabeth A. D. Eno

Dedicated to my father: the incomparable Adolphus Wong, who taught me unconditional love and how to give zero fucks. Miss you so.

CONTENTS

PREFACE ix

1. How I Trapped Your Father 3

2. The Miracle of Life 18

3. Tips on Giving Birth 33

4. Why I Went Back to Work 38

5. Hustle and Pho 47

6. Snake Heart 76

7. The DJ 103

8. Mr. Wong 109

9. A Guide to Asian Restaurants 126

10. Bringing Up Bébés 129

11. Uncle Andrew 141

12. My Least Favorite Question 155

13. Bridin' Dirty 171

14. Wild Child 182

AFTERWORD BY JUSTIN HAKUTA 197

ACKNOWLEDGMENTS 215

Why I'm Writing This Book

Dear Girls,
    I have a secret that I never wanted anyone to know. And no, it's not that I once slept with a homeless man (everybody already knows about that). Let me explain.

When I got this book deal, soon after the release of my first stand-up special, *Baby Cobra,* a deep panic set in. I immediately regretted signing the deal because I was terrified of the task at hand. I almost quit, conservatively, eighty times over the course of a year. A month before the first draft was due, I was moments away from giving the advance money back to the editor with a batch of balloons reading:

~~CONGRATULATIONS!~~ I QUIT! ¯_(ツ)_/¯

Yes, I'd been scared of the workload of writing a book. But really, I was more concerned that once I wrote it and published it, everyone would find out my secret—one that only my family and closest friends knew.

For three years, I was on the writing staff of the ABC sitcom *Fresh Off the Boat*. Every year, a producer-writer named Matt Kuhn would run a quiz before our annual staff trip to Vegas. It was meant to get us all excited about our brief escape from the fluorescent-lit office full of dry-erase boards, PC monitors, and bald white men in cargo shorts. One of my favorite questions was "Bronson Pinchot, the actor who played Balki Bartokomous from *Perfect Strangers:* dead or alive?" (spoiler: alive). The quiz was a mix of inside jokes and true, hardcore trivia.

One of the final questions in my second year on staff was "How many miles to the moon?" According to Google, it's about 238,900 miles. Every other staff member guessed somewhere in that ballpark.

My answer was five billion miles.

The looks on my co-workers' faces when they saw my terrifying guess, written on paper so there could be no mistaking it, are seared into my memory. One person took off her glasses and scream-laughed into an Ikea throw pillow for about five straight minutes. Another person just stared at me, plastered with a look of deep, sincere confusion as to how somebody so dense could have managed to graduate from college and get a job, let alone perform the basic functions of life such as remembering to breathe and wipe from front to back. It was like a bomb had exploded in the room and people suddenly suspected that there was a wizard operating my brain for my entire life and they caught a moment when he was on lunch break.

Some of my peers thought the answer was so ridiculous that I was just trying to be funny. But I wasn't trying to be funny. I was legitimately trying to win the quiz and get the cash prize of five hundred dollars to spend immediately upon landing in Vegas on buffets and VIP tickets to *Magic Mike Live*.

That day, my co-workers found out my secret: I'm a fucking idiot.

There are some major and wildly concerning gaps in my knowledge and abilities. I have a very hard time distinguishing an Australian person from a British person unless I get a good look in their mouth. No matter how many times someone explains it to me, I will never understand when to appropriately use "whom" instead of "who"—it's simply beyond my capabilities, sadly. My nephew beat me at chess in three moves when I was thirty and he was in preschool. Then I beat him in checkers (by cheating), I over-celebrated and gloated, and he gave me a look that said, "Wow, good for you," and waddled to the child's potty in his room to go poo. I do not know the difference between a crocodile and an alligator or a turtle and a tortoise or a sandwich and a panini. I believe it sounds like the ocean when you hold certain seashells up to your ear because you can take the seashell out of the ocean, but you can't take the ocean out of a seashell. I know that's not scientifically correct, but I'm too lazy to learn the real explanation behind the magic. I'm still not sure if Pluto is a planet or not, and I don't understand what a secretary of state does or why it's called a secretary (do they arrange FedEx pickups and have extramarital affairs with the state?). When a friend recently texted me that R. Kelly had been indicted, I had to google "What is the meaning of indicted?"

And so, with this published book, I was understandably afraid of the whole world knowing this. I confessed this to Sarah Dunn, author of *The Arrangement* and creator of the

ABC sitcom *American Housewife*. She told me, "Just accept that you're not a genius. Once I told myself that, I was able to finally write."

I felt so much better after my talk with her and got comfortable with the fact that I'm not Tolstoy. I'm not Salman Rushdie. Then I realized something better: Nobody expects me to be Salman Rushdie, or even Padma Lakshmi. (Hi, Padma, if you're reading! Love you on *Top Chef*! Quickfire queen!) And in all honesty, Salman Rushdie is boring and very difficult for the average person (me!) to get through without a teacher to guide one (me again!) through all the dense writing and big words. Also, up until recently, when I'd hear his name, I thought he was a type of fish.

I am not Maya Angelou. I am not Malcolm Gladwell. People shit on Dan Brown, and I'm no Dan Brown. Hell, I'm not even that fat mustache guy who faked his memoir and got yelled at by Oprah. I'm a stand-up comedian that's famous enough now to receive a free Nike tracksuit and get harassed for pictures when I go out to eat ramen. I'm a five-foot-tall girl from the San Francisco Bay who has always loved making people laugh. I got a 1200 on my SATs. I'm your mother. I don't write fancy. I don't use words like "facetious" or "effusive." I use words like "doo-doo," "caca," and "punani." Once I embraced that, these letters were an absolute pleasure to write.

The idea for this book is inspired mostly by a note from my father that began with "Dear Alexandra." He had left it for me in a sealed envelope before he passed away. He had been battling cancer and depression for a while, and he knew he was going to die soon. In it, he told me he loved me and promised I would have a great life. He thanked me for exercising with him in the park while he was sick and couldn't walk so well. I'm very grateful for the letter, but I wish he had written more about himself. There are so many questions I still have for him—about how he overcame all the challenges in his youth and about the person he was before I was born.

And so I wanted to leave something for you girls for when I die, besides a collection of oversized glasses for you to sell on eBay. These letters explore a lot of the topics I wish my father and I had discussed (and some I'm glad we didn't tbh). Then I figured, well, I should probably make money off them if I'm going to spend all this time writing them. I didn't want to just leave you with my stand-up specials that feature me, pregnant with you, shouting all of my opinions and grodie stories at strangers.

This book is also meant to address a lot of the questions I get asked by young people. Like, what is it like to be an Asian American woman in entertainment? How do you balance family and career? What is the key to being so tall and fabulous and knowledgeable about distances between planets?

Two things: First, do not read this book until you are over twenty-one. You should not be allowed to know these inappropriate things about me if you can't even buy beer yet. Second, if you have any questions after reading this book, you can always ask me, because I'm your mother and I plan on living until I'm two hundred. Also, because I'm your mother, most of this book will probably horrify you and you won't want to ask me about it. That might be a catch-22, I'm not googling it.

And if anyone else has questions, you have to wait until I get another book deal. Monetizing answers to FAQs is my new business model.

DEAR
GIRLS

CHAPTER 1

How I Trapped Your Father

Dear Girls,

Your dad is the (if we are divorced by the time you read this, please skip to the next sentence) best, but I didn't just find him overnight. In the fall of 2009, I had been living in NYC for a year and had been unlucky when it came to love and casual sex.

Well, let's just get right to it: I dated a series of men who had issues getting it up. It felt like a curse. Five guys in a row lost their boners in the middle of getting busy. Part of me blamed the Raynaud's disease, a condition that was passed on to me by my father. I have extremely poor circulation to my hands and feet, to the point where, in the cold, they will turn blue and feel like pain icicles. So, especially in the New York fall or wintertime, my bare hands, much like the hands of Rogue from the X-Men, could suck the life out of a man's erect penis.

After the first two guys that I hooked up with in NYC went soft on me, I grew extremely self-conscious of my White Walker fingers. By the third time I started making out with a new guy, I made sure to simultaneously warm my hands up by furiously rubbing them together and breathing into them like a homeless character in a theater production, next to a papier mâché trash-can fire.

I felt very good about this new method and used it on a man that I met through comedy friends at a bar. He lived in Coney Island. At the time, I was staying in SoHo, so he might as well have lived in Pyongyang. It took an hour and a half to get to his place by train, but it felt like three because we were both so horny.

He was extremely stupid. I know I've confessed that I'm no genius, but this guy had a lower back tattoo of Chinese characters, didn't know who Abraham Lincoln was (this is for real), and couldn't stop talking about how *The Crow* was the greatest movie ever made (it's good, however, *Clueless* is a masterpiece). But I hadn't gotten successfully laid in so long and was very eager to flex my new technique, so I made my way to Trash Island.

I'd thought the whole point of living far away in an outer borough was to afford yourself a nicer apartment with more space. This dude did have a queen-sized, four-poster bed, but . . . not in a good way. It was old and dusty and made me feel less like Elizabeth Bennet in *Pride and Prejudice* and more like that weird sick kid in *The Secret Garden* who sleeps in a tunic and is allergic to the sun. He passionately threw me onto the bed, but a sudden, deafening bed creak rendered the mood DOA. I would've believed him if he'd told me that a hundred people over the past two centuries had spent their final days dying of scurvy in this rickety, termite-infested bed.

His place was a shithole. But traveling to Coney Island is the New York subway ride equivalent of hiking Machu Picchu, and I'd reached the summit so I couldn't back down now.

On the train and all the way up until I grabbed his penis, I had been consistently rubbing my hands together to keep the blood flowing. And he stayed hard. My method was sound! We were ready to move to the next level and I was finally going to pork a man I met at a bar like those bitches did in *Sex and the City*. But as soon as he made first contact with my vagina—which Raynaud's *does not* affect—his boner melted into a wet Cheeto.

A total and oppressive silence filled the room. He didn't even apologize, offer to eat me out, or make me a sandwich, which I felt was quite rude. I wanted to go home, but I was too poor to take a cab back and it was way too late and unsafe to take the train by myself all the way back to SoHo. So I slept in this stranger's haunted Victorian bed for the rest of the night and left before I could learn his last name or get attacked by a ghost in a frilled puffy dress.

Sex and the City had promised me much more exciting casual sex in New York City. Before moving there, I was looking forward to spending the night in an art gallery curator's loft. Maybe his name was Demetri and he would make me post-coital French press coffee and poached eggs before I had to catch a taxi, in the same Vivienne Westwood dress and Manolo Blahnik heels from the night before, to my very important advertising job. Maybe Demetri was GREAT at eating ass and I would learn later at brunch with my sassy girlfriends that Demetri had, in fact, a reputation for being great at eating ass. Maybe he was known amongst power New York women as "the mASSter." Maybe eventually the relationship would peter out because he was *too good* at eating ass and my ass would get raw and I would get sick of this one-trick pony. I would try to do missionary with him and then he'd just turn me over, move his head down my butt, and then I'd think, *All this fucking dude does is eat ass.* And from that experience I would create the perfect slogan for the new "Yelp for Single Men" campaign and my advertising agency would make me executive girl boss president person!

Except I never got to sleep with anyone who earned more than fifteen dollars per hour during that first year in NYC. I'd consider myself a princess if any of the men owned a bed frame (even if it was full of bedbugs in powdered wigs). They never took me out on a date and all of them had roommates. That's what happens when you spontaneously go home with a fellow struggling stand-up comic or, even worse, an *impro-viser.* (Please always say "fuck no" to those "yes and" mother-fuckers.) At the time, I didn't require or need to be taken out to dinner. But after five consecutive pudding penises, I began to want to get to know a man a little more before taking a chance on his performance abilities. There was a lot on the line: I would have taken a sixth soft dick as a sign to give up my worldly possessions, shave my head, and make Buddha my husband.

What I really wanted was a boyfriend. The single life in New York was not just disappointing, it was lonely. Of course there's a ton of cool stuff to do there, but I got sick of seeing the latest MoMA exhibit by myself, eating delicious thin crust pizza by myself, and watching a homeless man argue with pigeons by myself.

On my first birthday in New York, I did three five-minute, unpaid sets. One in Bushwick, one on the Upper West Side, and the last on the Lower East Side. I told nobody it was my birthday. I didn't want people to feel bad for me, and I didn't want to acknowledge, even to myself, that this was what I was actually doing on my birthday, because I would have cried. I had already spent two of my post-college years backpacking through Asia solo, so I felt like I'd earned my Cheryl Strayed self-reflection-journey points and was ready for meaningful, caring companionship. I also craved a steady sexual partner, who knew all of my spots and gained a dedicated arsenal of no-fail moves, like pouring Fun Dip into my pussy and then going to town with that little sugar spoon, or sticking a wet thumb up my ass when I announce that I'm gonna cum, which, in my experience, works wonders on men as well. It's a bi-effective move that's rock-solid. Is "bi-effective" a word? Please look it up and let me know, I refuse to google anything for these letters.

It was exhausting, trying to train all of these new men who couldn't stay hard. And I got tired of masturbating in my NYC loft, quietly and sans vibrator so as to not disturb my sixty-seven-year-old Russian landlady/roommate. The low rent she charged allowed me to be one of the only struggling stand-ups who could afford to live in Manhattan, and I wasn't about to fuck it up with some loud-ass vibrator just because I was too impatient to masturbate Amish-style.

In the fall of 2009, my old high school friend Abby Goldberg invited me to her wedding. At the time, I was twenty-seven years old and she was my very first friend to get married. Her grandfather co-ran a major felt company. Yes, that's what we mean when we say white people are beginning from a different starting line than everyone else. No matter how hard you study or work, you cannot compete with someone when their grandparents manufactured motherfucking *felt,* a material so iconic that even you two girls could recognize it by the age of one. Your Mickey Mouse ears wouldn't exist without Abby's family. It had never occurred to me that someone even *could* make felt; I must have subconsciously decided that, like a pen or a paper clip, it just occurs naturally.

The two-hundred-fifty-plus-guest Jewish wedding at a Napa vineyard was the most lavish nuptials I had ever been to. Most of the weddings I have attended since have a three-hour time limit on the free alcohol. The bat signal goes out to the guests that the open bar is about to close, and people savagely race to the bar, like those shitty-ass buffalos who trampled all over Mufasa in *The Lion King*, to get their last glass of complimentary booze to hold them over for the rest of the evening. This wedding had an open bar starting *before* the ceremony, well after the dinner, and the cocktails had all sorts of delicious, fresh-squeezed peach juices and tasted like decorative pillows from Anthropologie. The guests consisted mostly of Jewish people. So right away, I took notice of the only other Asian person at the wedding: your father.

I thought he was very, *very* handsome and was excited to learn that he had gone to high school with the groom. Bingo! A fellow private school Asian American! I have always loved Asian American men (despite my pussy's non-discriminatory, open-door policy), and I hope you end up with an Asian American man or woman as well. In fact, it would be wonderful if you could end up with an Asian American woman and don't have to weather through any bummer boners. There are *a lot* of advantages to being with someone of your own race. The cultural shorthand makes it a lot easier. You don't have to constantly explain everything or act like a smiling tour guide for Asian American culture or deal with dietary differences. I hate going out to eat Asian food with non-Asian people, especially dim sum, because there are *so many* dishes that they have *so many* questions about.

"What is that?"

"Ew, what is *that*?"

"What the FUCK IS that???"

"Is any of this organic?"

"Why do all these entrees have eyes??"

"Damn, you're really gonna eat feet?!!!"

I feel like what they're really asking is: "Why is that not a sandwich?" My response over the years has evolved to: "It's all pork and shrimp. Just eat it." I didn't drive all the way to this strip mall in Monterey Park or take the train all the way to Flushing to become your dim sum mentor. The worst is when non-Asian people call chicken's feet or pig's feet "nasty," because they're insulting the food I grew up on, that I'm excited to order and eat. My people used this food to nourish themselves and one another, and you're calling it disgusting. I know I'm on a tangent—I think I have PTSD from when I was one of the few Asian kids in kindergarten and all the white kids made fun of my "smelly" and "weird" lunch. And now that we're all grown up, those same white kids (I mean *literally* the same people) like to post pics of their chimichurri bone marrow dish, and I'm like, *Bitch, you used to call me a fucking vulture for eating my meat to the bone and sucking out the marrow. Now you're fishing for "Likes" with it??*

Non-Asian men I dated loved to brag about how "down" with Asian cuisine they were. One actually said to me enthusiastically, "I eat kimchi!" In my head I was thinking, *Bro, that is the staple of Korean cuisine. That's like me bragging to white people that I can identify with them because I eat bread.* You would think that I would've dumped him after that, but he paid for drinks and I wanted to squeeze just one more free meal out of him because, truthfully, I love kimchi. And besides, a man who's down to eat fermented cabbage is also probably down to eat butt after a long, humid summer day. Probiotics!

Also, when you date a fellow Asian American, the hygiene standards are generally much more aligned. My Asian American friends automatically take off their shoes at the entrance of my home. But with other people I always have to police them right when they come in the door and remind them to do it the next time and basically every time they come over. They never remember! What do I gotta do? Tattoo "Take your damn shoes off" on their arm like in *Memento*? And when they ask *why,* my response is *why the hell not?* Sorry if I don't want you dragging the gross shit you stepped on today into my clean home. I didn't vacuum and swiffer my floors so you could spread crackhead doo-doo and rat placentas all over them.

Asian men are also *extremely* attractive. I grew up in San Francisco where there were plenty of Asian men to choose from. There are Asian American women who proudly proclaim they do not date Asian men. They are not just snobs, but probably grew up way too isolated from fellow Asian Americans and believe the same stereotypes about us that mainstream America does: That we are boring; that we are great at STEM but not so great at anything involving creativity and actual excitement; that our men are robot nerds who have no idea how to find a woman's clitoris. But I am an Asian woman with an Asian fetish for Asian men. Have you seen their cheekbones?? Asian men are basically those blue Na'vi people from *Avatar,* only without the magic sex braids (although there was one guy . . .). If you want a great example of what I'm saying, try searching Google images for "Daniel Dae Kim," the actor from that TV show *Lost*. He's so sexy that I had Netflix spend a bunch of money on a movie I co-wrote called *Always Be My Maybe* just to give me an excuse to kiss him. That guy looks like a statue, and girls, so does your father. I saw him at that wedding and thought he resembled Keanu Reeves. Not *The Matrix* Keanu. Not *John Wick* Keanu. I'm talking *Speed* Keanu.

At the end of the wedding, I interrupted a conversation your father was having with an old friend so I could introduce myself. The only intel I'd been able to get on him at the wedding was that he was also living in NYC and very into health and wellness.

Me: "Hi, I'm Ali, I'm an old high school friend of Abby's. I heard you're a vegan, I'm sorta vegan as well." [Lies. I had salmon and beef that very night at the wedding!]

Your Dad: "Oh really? Cool. This is an old high school friend of me and Scott's, Kevin—"

Me, not giving a fuck about Kevin and wishing Kevin would go away already: "So where do you live now? I'm in New York. I heard you're living in New York too? I cook a lot of vegan food. Like amaranth. It helps keep me regular."

Your Dad: "Oh, that's great."

Me, panicking that this is not going well: "Anyway, I love yoga too. Do you ever go to Yoga to the

People? It's like communist yoga. Donation based.
Each according to his abilities. I love deep breathing."

Your Dad: "Me too. You know, Kevin and I haven't
seen each other in a long time so—"

Me, with flop sweat going for a Hail Mary: "Yeah,
I have very important old people to talk to as well.
Abby's grandma and everything. Listen, I'm a stand-
up comic and why don't I get your email so you can
come to one of my shows if you're free or whatever?"

Your Dad, starting to turn away: "Yeah, sure."

It wasn't great. But I knew that the only way to get him
eventually was with my wit and humor because in terms of
looks, he was a little out of my league.

Soon after the Napa wedding, I emailed him an invite to a
show that I was headlining at Gotham Comedy Club in NYC.
If you can believe it, I was a way dirtier comedian then. I used
to do a joke where I'd do an impression of an animated e-
card. I'd hum "Row Row Row Your Boat" while doing "the
robot" and making a cartoonishly happy face. Then I'd turn
around, bend over, and pull my pants down to show the
whole audience my bare ass, and say, *"What's crackin'?!"*

You know, smart people stuff.

Sometimes I would pull my pants a little too far down,
and I'm sure the audience could see my untrimmed pubes
hanging from the other side, like some faraway tumbleweed.
I didn't really care if they saw it or not. I've always thought
it's much more embarrassing for people to see a giant zit on
your nose than your bushy vag. Anyway, it was a very incom-

plete joke and basically an excuse to moon the audience. Another one of my early classics was: "Last night I mixed up the toothpaste with the K-Y Jelly, and I woke up with an extra white butthole."

It was a gamble inviting your father to that show but I already knew, since I had met him through a high school connection, that we had some sort of potential. If we did get together I didn't want it to be just a one-night stand, and I didn't want to surprise him later on with my crazy. I liked to get the message that I was an untamable spirit out right away. It's like that old saying: If you can't handle me when I show you my gaping butthole, you don't deserve the rest of me. Or however it goes.

Anyway, the risk paid off—your dad saw my ass and pubes on a stage surrounded by strangers and emailed me immediately after the show, telling me that he hadn't laughed that hard in a while. In his email, he wrote, "My hands were buzzing." It's still one of the oddest things anyone has said to me in response to my comedy, and made me question whether he might have Raynaud's disease too. But I took it as a compliment, because he invited me to have lunch with him.

He suggested we meet at a restaurant that does not exist anymore because it never should have existed in the first place. It was called Home but it didn't make me think of home. It made me think of drowning myself in a bowl of tom yum soup. It served pan-Asian cuisine and made Panda Express look like a Michelin-starred restaurant. I looked at Yelp and the pictures of the food all featured those carrots that are cut into rhombuses with ridges. Here's a little piece of advice: Those carrots are always an indicator that you are about to eat some frozen shit food prepared by the dirty hands of people who could give two fucks about it. Sucker customers ordered, paid, and then picked up their food at the counter. It was cash only. And guess what? Your dad didn't have any cash on him. It was only after he insisted I order first, didn't pay for my food, and ordered his own dish that he realized his wallet was completely empty—that kind of empty where a puff of dust and disappointment wafts out. He laughed, asked to borrow money from me, and after I handed him the cash, made this joke: "I'm like Nicolas Cage in that movie *The Weather Man*!"

Like every human on Earth except him, I didn't get it. It was a reference to an obscure 2005 film starring Nicolas Cage and Michael Caine. I'm extremely confident that Nicolas Cage and Michael Caine wouldn't have gotten the reference either. I had never seen it before, just like how I had never eaten at that filthy nutsack of a restaurant before. I guess one way to look at it was that your dad was introducing me to all sorts of new things? Daddy's "joke" was referencing a scene where Nicolas Cage doesn't have a quarter for a paper and his father, played by Michael Caine, tells him he is a grown man who should carry more than a dollar.

I wore a dress and shaved my legs for this? I was hoping to show him a softer, more feminine side of myself. Daddy came to this lunch dressed in black Lululemon pants and an electric-blue Lululemon shirt with his yoga mat slung over his shoulder in a yoga mat case, like a Santa Monica trophy wife running errands.

I would've accepted and maybe even embraced his outfit choice had the whole date not started with him not paying. I feel very strongly that men should have to pay, at least for the first date. Paying for the first date is to compensate for all the time and money women are expected to spend on themselves just to get ready for that date. It's the same reason why men should be the ones to propose to the woman and buy her the ring. It shows initiative, which is so important for a woman like myself, who has had to jump-start so much in her own life. Paying for the first date sets a precedent that says, "I want to take care of you. I want to provide for you." And no, I don't expect a man to take care of me financially, but I want him to want to, to take the opportunity, to make the gesture of doing something nice and giving right away.

Well, your father, choosing a terrible restaurant, borrowing money from me, and then outing himself as a Nicolas Cage fan, did not seize any opportunity to show that he was a man capable of making caring decisions. I don't even remember what we talked about as I ate my plate of orange chicken lo mein from a red plastic cafeteria tray. I was in such a bad mood that I made a point to not hug him or say "see you soon" when it was all over.

Neither of us made contact after that. I did not want him to call me again, unless it was to deposit $32.51 into my bank account. I was so fed up with these men in New York who just kept disappointing me via their penises and/or lack of chivalry. Was it really too much to ask to find *one* courteous man with a working penis in all of New York?

Then I ran into your dad on the street, weeks later. He was in that same blue yoga top and black pants, with the same yoga mat slung over his shoulder. And I was reminded of how handsome he was, with that chiseled face and that sexy deep voice. And how he had such a powerful, gentle energy and was into health and wellness and how the main thing everyone said about him was that he was "wicked smart." (People on the East Coast have the oddest slang. It's hella strange.)

So Daddy contacted Mommy once again.

He took me out to lunch at a Japanese teahouse and declared at the beginning of the meal that he was going to pay since he owed me. I ordered the most expensive dish possible: the black cod bowl. For reparations. It was a much better restaurant and we had a much better conversation.

He asked me: "If you could have any superpower, what would it be?"

Right away, I answered: "To speak every language in the world."

His jaw dropped and he asked: "Are you joking? Are you kidding me?"

Me: "If I was, that wouldn't be a very funny joke."

Him: "Well, that's crazy because that would be my superpower too."

We talked about living abroad in college, his work in the Philippines when he was a Fulbright scholar, and connecting to the countries where our mothers were born and raised.

For our third date, I suggested we go to Yoga to the People, that donation-based yoga class in the East Village I had mentioned at the wedding. Since we were both into health and wellness, it was really nice to do that kind of activity together, and just see each other sweat through our clothing, and put all the pheromones fully out there before even getting intimate. It's always challenging not to fart during yoga, but that day, I clenched my cheeks extra tight during happy baby pose. By that point I knew I liked him more than

any of those dudes who had dead koala arms dangling between their legs, and decided to go in for the kill: I made him
a vegan meal. Peanut noodles with spicy tofu and garlic Chinese broccoli. He was entranced. I had officially trapped
his ass.

On our fifth date, he finally took me out to dinner at a
restaurant called Caravan of Dreams, also located in the East
Village. Afterward, he walked me back to my apartment in
SoHo and kissed me on the stoop. It was magical, which I
know sounds corny but you two are still into Disney prin-
cesses right now, so don't judge me. It wasn't Harry Potter
magical or turning a soft penis hard (and making it stay that
way!) magical. This was *real* magic, a spark and a connection
that I felt deep down inside of me. I can still see the sweatshirt he was wearing, which had a corduroy moose sewn onto
it. On that grimy New York street full of trash bag mountains, it made me feel like I was in a ski lodge next to a fire,
looking out at snowy mountains. It also made me feel like he
needed some better clothes, besides that blue yoga top and
this forest camel sweatshirt. He only ever wore those two
things. He still has the moose sweatshirt, and I hope he never
gives it away.

A few years later, your father proposed to me on that exact
same apartment stoop on Greene Street. Nearby, a homeless
man was arguing with a pigeon. We both witnessed it together. And I knew I would never have to be by myself ever
again.

CHAPTER 2

The Miracle of Life

Dear Girls,
     Even before your father and I got married, I felt like it was time to start trying for a baby. I had family and friends go through expensive and grueling fertility treatments. Some were successful and some weren't, but they all told me the same thing: that they regretted trying too late. I came from a family with four kids and my intention was to have four of my own. I loved growing up in a big family. Our dynamic was very similar to that of the Pfeffermans in *Transparent,* but with less Havdalah ceremonies and more dried squid. The house was full of laughter, opinions, yelling, tension, and first-world problems. My dad would sometimes say things to my mom like, "Devil, get away, for I am God's property!" And at my age, I still cannot find anyone, besides my siblings, who can relate to having a dad who would clap back at his wife like a crazy gold miner from the 1800s. In his

defense, it's a bulletproof line to use in a fight. What is the comeback to that?

My father passed away when I was twenty-seven years old, and I couldn't imagine having to deal with his death without every single one of my siblings. Without the four of us, my mom would have been all alone to deal with her grief, the logistics of the funeral (choosing a casket is very overwhelming), and then the rest of her life. Asian women live forever, and having kids is like a 401(k) for companionship. When you two inevitably become widows for the second hundred years of your lives, you're going to need some progeny to care about you and, most important, to owe you.

I try to imagine my mom's life now without her children and grandchildren. Being an adult is scary, especially if and when you lose your lifetime partner. Her house is already borderline Asian *Grey Gardens,* but it would be exponentially worse if my siblings and I didn't exist. We are the ones who hook up and fix her Internet, force her to get rid of the gigantic *Encyclopaedia Britannica* set, replace the green 1970s refrigerator, and throw away the expired antibiotics. We take turns listening to her ramble about all of the juicy Asian American elderly gossip (which basically consists of who is dead, and who should be but isn't). The worst part about being the child of an immigrant is that you have to help your mother switch her cellphone plan. "Mom! For the tenth time, I'm telling you, DO NOT GO WITH CRICKET!!!" My white friends have to offer some amount of tech help to their aging parents, but for some reason, none of them are involved in their parents' cellphone provider decisions. And as agonizing as that process and all of the other things I've done for my mother are, it's nothing in comparison to what she has given me.

I really romanticized being pregnant from a young age. I

loved stuffing dolls up my shirt to pretend there was a baby in my belly (since we lived in less woke times it was always a blond-haired, blue-eyed baby). When I was in eighth grade, we dissected frogs in biology class. Their poor bodies were so cold and slimy, and the chemicals used to preserve them made me dizzy. My classmates and I were much more interested in looking at pictures of Luke Perry (RIP) than snipping through the belly of a dead amphibian. Our science teacher, Mrs. Landers, was seven months pregnant at the time. She excused herself from the classroom when the frogs arrived, because she said breathing in the formaldehyde was potentially harmful to her baby. She tagged in the vegan art teacher who was just as repulsed as we were. I thought, *Wow, being pregnant can get you out of a lot of stuff.*

I was also very motivated to have you as soon as possible because I didn't want to be an old parent. When I was born, my mom was forty-two and my dad was forty-seven. They both went gray almost immediately and used to dye each other's hair black. It was really cute watching them squeeze the tube of cheap hair dye goo purchased from 99 Ranch Market onto the special comb and apply it to each other's hair, each with a big beach towel wrapped around their shoulders. They always seemed so giddy to age each other down. But when you have old parents, you're always scared they're going to die and you never feel protected. When I was in second grade, my dad hurt his back and started walking with a cane that had a gold duck's head for the handle. I think gripping onto a lower life-form's cranium for support made him feel a lot more empowered about getting old, like, *I'm still doing better than this poor fucking thing. Now, support my weight, duck!* I have no memories of my parents going down a slide or riding a roller coaster with me. By the time I was born they were too scared of hurting themselves and out-sourced those activities to my older siblings.

When my dad was sick with cancer, he, like a lot of sick people, took his frustration and anger out on his caretaker: my mom. He was not himself and, in his delirious state, told me: "I was so mad when I found out Mom was pregnant with you, because it was yet another sign of her neglect—that she had forgotten to take her birth control pill." I didn't say anything back to my dad, because I knew he was just expressing how angry he was that he was physically weak, that he was dying. He couldn't drive anymore, he couldn't go to the bathroom by himself anymore. It was all very disempowering. At his funeral, a family friend felt the need to tell me how upset my mom was when she found out she was pregnant with me: "I remember your mom coming out of the sauna, with a towel wrapped around her head and body, and saying to me with a frown, so grumpily, 'I'm pregnant.'" I told the family friend, "You've told me that story already. I don't know why you keep telling it to me." (Translation: "Write some new material, bitch!") Sometimes I feel like a lot of my motivation comes from a need to prove to my parents that they should be gladder they had me.

Unlike me, neither of you were accidents. You were very much wanted and planned. You were so planned, in fact, that the intense scheduling of ovulation sex pretty much ruined sex instantly, so, you're welcome.

I wanted to have kids close in age because the gap between me and my siblings was painful. They were all ten to fifteen years older than I was and had lived a whole different life as a family of five before I was born. There are framed pictures of them, all on skis. By the time I was born, my parents weren't hitting the slopes; they were hitting the Metamucil. (To be fair, I gave up on skiing because I crashed into a tree while trying to conquer a half-pipe when I was eleven years old so please don't expect Mommy to ski with you ever.) It was traumatizing when my siblings all went to college. I played in the closet with all my stuffed animals because I didn't want to feel the void of my missing sister Mimi, who up until that point I had always shared a room with.

When I was in third grade, Mimi used to pick me up from school in her gray Volvo station wagon, and I climbed in the back, illegally sitting on the laps of her volleyball teammates. All of my classmates, uniformed in green plaid jumpers over white blouses and brown shoes, watched in envy as I drove away in a car full of supercool teenage girls. At Mels Drive-In, I felt so empowered to choose my own dish (fish sticks don't really qualify as a "dish" but the point here is *empowerment*), because we always ate family style at Chinese restaurants and my parents always ordered. And before sliding into the squeaky red booth, Mimi gave me a quarter for the jukebox. I selected "Everyday" by Buddy Holly—*Stand by Me* was my favorite movie because River Phoenix was the hottest boy of all time to a third-grader born in 1982. All of her friends exclaimed, "Great choice, Alexandra!" as I sat back down and smiled while coloring with the provided crayons, listening to them talk about Madonna and boys, riveted by all of it. So when she went away to college, suddenly there was nobody to take me to the disgusting non-Chinese restaurants I wanted to eat at, like Mels Drive-In. I missed her friends. I missed her letting me choose. I hated seeing her empty bed, I missed her piles of clothes everywhere on the floor.

I missed Mimi.

———

I was thirty-one years old when Daddy and I decided to try for a family. We used these one hundred for ten dollars ovulation strips on Amazon. They came from China, packaged in a cheap ziplock bag with no instructions. After one month of aforementioned scheduled sex, I was pregnant. I was so happy and told all of my friends, my family, my co-workers, and lots and lots of strangers. Then eleven weeks into the pregnancy, I started spotting.

That night I had a miscarriage. Now I know why you're supposed to wait until after the first trimester to tell people that you're pregnant. It's very rude to ask a woman if she's pregnant or if she's trying because you have no idea how long or how hard she's tried or if it's a conversation she's even had with her partner. If she is pregnant, that might not be information she's ready to share. If you end up having a miscarriage (which is *very* common), you don't want to then be forced to tell everyone the bad news. I couldn't believe some of the insensitive responses I got when I told people about my loss. Here are the top five:

1. WHY?

2. Well, did you take folic acid?

3. It was probably from all the performing.

4. Was it because you were stressed out?

5. Was the doctor able to determine the cause?

Or in other words, "Hey, Ali, how'd you manage to fuck up your pregnancy??" The underlying message of those reactions suggested there was blame to be placed on me, as if I had control of the very unfortunate outcome. When you go through something as tragic as a miscarriage, the last thing you want is to feel like it was your fault. I didn't want to share with anyone what had happened because I was scared they would think my body was fundamentally defective. And I also didn't want to bum people out. It's very hard to tell someone you had a miscarriage and then casually go back to eating hand-pulled noodles and talking shit about the latest comedians getting into a Twitter battle. Here's my tip for the best thing to say when someone tells you she miscarried: "I'm so sorry to hear that." That's *all you have to say*. Other responses I would've appreciated are: "How are you feeling?" or "I know so many women who have had a miscarriage, and it sucks, but you're not alone" or "Here's a frozen bag of dumplings my Shanghainese mom who used to have a dumpling shop in Shanghai made."

It helps so much to know you're not the only one who has had one, because then you realize it's not your fault. Miscarriages don't discriminate, and there is nothing I could've done. I found great comfort in knowing that Beyoncé also miscarried. If the goddess queen had a miscarriage, it's okay that I had one too. In fact, we were part of a special club now. Actually, now it's like I'm friends with Beyoncé. And by extension I am now besties with HOV, Michelle (spoiler alert: She had a miscarriage too and writes about it in her awesome book) and Barack, and nobody understands what it's like to be us, right? That's what I'll say in the deposition when I get arrested for hugging them to death. It is one thing to hear the statistic that one in four pregnancies will result in a miscarriage. But it's another thing to put faces to actual women who have experienced the same loss, like the beautiful face of my BFF Beyoncé. Because I was forced to be so open about having a miscarriage, women privately shared their own personal stories of loss and I remember every single one.

After that I did my best to convert my grief into a celebration of my unexpected but suddenly extended independence. I decided to view it as a bonus round of opportunities, to do whatever I wanted. That is to say, I discovered the joy of edibles. Every weekend, I'd eat a weed gummy, watch a Hayao Miyazaki movie, blissfully sink into the couch, and eat sashimi. It was like an awesome bachelorette party where I didn't have to leave my house and the maid of honor was an animated Japanese cat-bus.

―――――

Three months after the miscarriage, I got pregnant again with Mari. This time, I made sure not to tell anyone until I was four months in. The miscarriage colored all of my decisions and attitude during the pregnancy. Every day of every trimester was filled with happiness that I was still carrying and paranoia that I could all of a sudden lose the baby. So I never got too upset about all the discomfort. Even when I was throwing up on planes, even when I would get a charley horse at night that felt like a ghost was strangling my calf, I was just grateful Mari was alive. I didn't mind the weight gain either. Looking pregnant was a privilege and so was getting to wear maternity clothes. It was liberating to not have to worry about sucking in my belly or selecting outfits that would make my stomach look flatter. Most of the time I rocked tight dresses that would make me look even more pregnant to capitalize on strangers opening doors for me and offering to carry anything heavy.

After a while, I couldn't see my vagina when I looked

down, because all I could see was my belly. But when I stared at myself in the mirror, my vagina just looked like an ancient, wise Chinese man from a fairy tale that got stuck in a cave and survived off yams. The hair was so damn long and neglected. My nipples became progressively bigger and darker. One day I noticed the tips were starting to look a little scaly and naturally rubbed them. Some bits started to flake off like tiny brown boogers. And I just sat on the bathroom floor completely naked, with a garbage can between my thighs, picking at my nipples. Daddy walked in on me while I was completely focused on this important activity and asked, "Are you harvesting your nipples?" I didn't even look at him and just responded, "Well, obviously."

Before I got pregnant, I was determined to have a kumbaya hippie birth in water, surrounded by a Santa Monica sorceress named Owlfeathers and lots of chanting. One TV director gave me her meditation CDs that were meant to guide you through an epidural-free labor. (Fun fact: You can't meditate your cervix to open wider so don't waste your time!) Another mom told me that when she felt the baby coming, she squatted at home and then pulled the baby's head out from her vagina, all by herself. Which is cool and independent and everything, but like, be humble. One friend posted an Instagram picture of her naked, looking orgasmic, in a tub sitting on her husband's lap, with her newborn baby covered in fresh afterbirth lying on her chest. They all made it seem so easy, natural, and *fun*! I made plans to eat my placenta to prevent postpartum depression and not waste any of that valuable, free nutrition (if you haven't picked up on it by now, I'm extremely cheap).

But I had to let go of the magical unknown moment of

"going into labor" when the doctor let me know, at thirty weeks, that Mari wasn't growing enough. I had a condition called intrauterine growth restriction (IUGR), which affects 10 percent of pregnant women. Apparently there was some blood flow resistance in the umbilical cord from the placenta to Mari. It was unsafe for her to stay in my womb past thirty-seven weeks at the very latest, and my obstetrician explained that she would get better nutrition outside rather than staying inside. This did not help my paranoia. One day, I didn't feel the baby kick for three hours. A co-worker told me that drinking a little bit of orange juice could stimulate baby movement. So I decided to chug a can of grape soda just to be safe, and lay down on the floor in my windowless office, underneath my desk where it was quiet and dim, so I could put my hands on my belly and focus on feeling my baby's tiny feet and fists, which would give me relief that she was still alive. Staring at the legs of my cold metal desk, the quiet and stillness of my body was terrorizing me. Also all that sugar from the grape soda, which I hadn't drunk since I was a kid, was making me feel like someone was prying my eyes open. I lay there on my side for a good five minutes and almost started to cry when all of a sudden Mari turned into a Muay Thai kickboxer defending her title as the strongest, sweetest baby. And instead of crying, I just laughed. I laughed and laughed, all by myself, underneath that desk, lying on that dirty-ass gray carpet.

I didn't want to tell anyone about my condition but then people kept on asking about my due date. So I had to explain that we were most likely going to have to get induced at thirty-seven weeks or get a C-section. When I told people, their faces would wince and they would ask me a bunch of questions that rang a bell:

1. WHY?

2. Is it because you ate old leftovers?

3. It was probably from all the performing.

4. Was it because you were stressed out?

5. Was the doctor able to determine the cause?

As if I didn't feel enough shame, these questions only made me feel worse. Again. I felt like people were judging my body to be fundamentally flawed. But unlike the miscarriage, this was not as common and at the time I didn't know anybody else who had this condition. There was no Beyoncé lighthouse to show me the way. Mari had been inside of me, growing and kicking, for seven and a half months. I already loved her so much, could not stand the thought of losing her, and would never have had the emotional strength to try getting pregnant again if something tragic happened. Plus, I had just taped my very first stand-up special pregnant. How would people be able to laugh at my jokes if the baby they were watching inside didn't survive? It would have turned that special into an avant-garde tragedy.

I had to go to the hospital twice a week for "perinatal testing," to make sure Mari was okay and wouldn't have to come out sooner than thirty-seven weeks. A nurse would hook me up to a monitor to check the baby's heartbeat and my amniotic fluid, while I tried to decide which celebrity "wore it best" in the latest issue of *Us Weekly*. According to the perinatal nurses, most patients found it to be a nuisance but I loved getting to listen to Mari's heartbeat. Because of the miscarriage I was filled with anxiety about Mari's survival, so I was ecstatic and relieved to confirm she was still okay.

I made it to thirty-seven weeks and they tried to induce me. I had contractions for twenty-four hours but my cervix was still only dilated half a centimeter. It hurt like hell because I was trying to push a cantaloupe out of a hole the size of an apple stem. The doctor offered to put some medical balloon up my pussy to open up the cervix more, which to me sounded like some sort of interrogation torture tactic. Clowns have always scared me and while I've slept with two homeless people, I really didn't want to get fucked by a balloon. Despite the nurse's discouragement, I decided to go straight to the C-section. It was the first lesson in having kids: You cannot control anything. Whatever dreams you had of how things were going to go down, they ain't gonna come true. Kiss goodbye your fantasy of delivering your baby in a rain forest, or in a Buddhist temple surrounded by frangipani flowers, and get ready to shit your pants emotionally and physically.

In the morning the nurse came in to shave my pussy. I wasn't able to trim or even see my own vagina for the last four months of my pregnancy, so it was a nice reunion with myself. But the pile of hair she had cut off looked like a New York rat. And it didn't get shaved again until the second time I had a C-section. And then I was rolled into the operating room without Daddy. The room was so bright and sterile, no kind of place at all for a proper balloon fucking. I had made the right choice.

The anesthesiologist discovered I had scoliosis and then proceeded to attempt to search for a spot on my twisted spine. He missed with the needle about a million times— every time he guessed wrong he said out loud, very casually, "Well, that's not it." All of the bloody tissues were piling up around me and I started sobbing. The anesthesiologist asked me in disbelief, "Are you crying?" and I screamed, "Yes, I'm crying!" Here's a free tip for anesthesiologists: If your patient is crying, you're bad at anesthesiology. He finally got the needle in and I felt a rush of warmth through the bottom half of my body. Daddy was escorted into the operating room, to find me shaking from the drugs, with my teeth wildly chattering. He took my hand, and I pulled his ear right up to my mouth and said, "We are never doing this again." Like a good man, he said, "Okay."

But ten minutes later, Mari came out, and I saw her cute little face above the curtain and immediately said to Daddy, "Let's do it again." Like a good man, he said, "Okay."

And then I threw up from all the anesthesia and my teeth were still chattering and they were telling me not to vomit so hard, otherwise my stitches would bust open. I said, "I don't know how to vomit softly." That's like telling someone to shit perfume.

Some women want to maintain mystique by making sure that the husband doesn't look beyond the curtain. Well, your daddy looked anyway. He saw my spleen, my intestines, and all the other guts down there that I'm not educated enough to identify. And I'm glad he saw them. Because now he knows that he owes me forever. Also, it's very hard to divorce somebody once you know what their spleen looks like. It doesn't get much more intimate than that. I regularly pull the "C-section card" whenever I want to get out of a household chore. If he asks me to unload the dishwasher, I just say, "Sure, I'll do that when you've gone through this." And then I make a slicing motion below his belly button while screaming aggressive karate noises, and he'll immediately start putting away the clean plates and utensils. The C-section was an odd blessing in mandating more shared parenting responsibility. I didn't change a single diaper for the two weeks Daddy was on paternity leave since I could barely walk. In the two months following Mari's birth, my incision got infected twice, and my ob-gyn mandated that I rest more. Daddy had no choice but to get up with me in the middle of the night when I had to feed the baby. Unlike some fathers, he had to soothe Mari and swaddle her and get to know her and *be a parent*.

Mari was a great distraction from the C-section recovery, and I experienced no pain. I was also taking a lot of Vicodin. On further analysis, it was likely more due to the Vicodin. At first I felt guilty about taking it while breastfeeding but then I talked to my pharmacist friend Aileen, who had just had a C-section with twins a month earlier. Her response to my questions about the safety of it was: "You have suffered enough." That became my mantra for motherhood from there on out.

You have suffered enough.

If you can make it easier, *make it easier,* and don't feel guilty about it.

Plus I think the Vicodin helped Mari sleep better.

Then I did it all again with Nikki but it was better because I knew what to expect. Also the anesthesiologist for Nikki was so much more nurturing and got my spine on the first try because she paid attention in medical school. Maybe looking her in the eye before the surgery and telling her, "If you miss my fucking spine I will write all about how you missed my fucking spine in my upcoming book *Dear Girls*" helped as well.

My dream of having four children was replaced by utter gratitude that I was able to get pregnant three times, and give birth to two beautiful girls, who exhaust me spiritually, financially, and emotionally.

I came to see that everything really does happen for a reason. If I hadn't had that miscarriage, you, my dear Mari, never would've been born. And as I write this letter, Nikki is sleeping in her swing chair, one month old. I am wearing a diaper because I still have afterbirth leaking out of my pussy. My breasts are veiny and engorged with milk, my shirt has baby-shit stains, and I am so tired that I feel like I've been swimming in the ocean for twenty days straight.

But it's worth it.

(Mostly.)

CHAPTER 3

Tips on Giving Birth

Dear Girls,
     Here are a few quick tips on the hospital stay, when and if you give birth:

1. **Bring Depends for yourself.** It made all the difference the second time around. You don't want to be stuck with that hospital mega-pad that is constantly slipping and sliding in that mesh underwear. What you want is a nice flesh-tone adult diaper, with a pad built in to the underwear. No adhesive needed! Like one of those awesome push-up bras where the chicken cutlets are just sewn into the bra!

2. **Bring a breastfeeding pillow.** The first time around, I had to stack up tiny hospital pillows underneath my forearms to provide support. It was a very un-ergonomic

assault on my back and shoulders. I brought wrist guards the second time around as well. I looked like a member of the Cobra Kai, but it was worth it. Also, everyone kept asking me if I had carpal tunnel, and I was like, *Bitch, I'm doing this because I* don't want *carpal tunnel.*

3. Don't get tricked into paying for the bigger birthing suite that's three hundred dollars more per night. I liked being in a small room, where the bed was close to the bathroom. After you give birth you're very constipated so they put you on milk of magnesia and stool softeners that make you have wild diarrhea, and you want to be as close to the bathroom as possible so you don't shit your pants. The downside is that when you have visitors and need to blow it up in the bathroom, they'll hear you blowing it up in the bathroom. But you shouldn't be inviting people to meet the new baby right away if you're not comfortable with them seeing your boobs or listening to your volcanic asshole.

4. Bring a nice blanket, something soft and cozy that feels like the inside of an Ugg boot or a Care Bear's vagina. Hospital bedding does not spark joy. The sheets have a thread count of three and there's always some sort of plastic lining underneath to protect the mattress from all the new moms leaking juice everywhere. It made me feel like a patient in *One Flew Over the Cuckoo's Nest.* If you haven't seen that movie, turn off the phone in your eyeball (or whatever technology you have now) and watch it. It's way stressful but amazing!

5. Bring DVDs or an HDMI cable for your laptop.
It was really fun for me and Daddy to watch movies in
the hospital, and it made the whole experience feel
more like a vacation. A vacation where your body ex-
plodes, but still, you're not at the office. And new-
borns are great but they're not that exciting after a
while (ten minutes), especially when they're attached
to your boob and you can't use your hands at all. Do
not bring any books though. You will have zero brain
cells for reading, pretty much ever again.

6. Pack lots of snacks. Your favorite snacks. Hospital food is a funeral of flavor in your mouth. They just
steam sliced carrots and white chicken breasts and
then shove a little cup of red Jell-O at you and expect
you to be happy. Which you should be, because that
bland-ass food means the hospital is doing its job.
They're putting all of their energy into keeping people alive while not getting sued. If a hospital has great
food it's probably a terrible hospital. Good food takes
a lot of focus, and I would rather that focus was on
me and my erupting body, and not on whether fava
beans make a good side dish for dry-rubbed cumin
lamb.

7. Bring a cute-ass onesie for the baby. It will make
you love the baby more (which is very important when
they need to clamp onto your breast like titty-milk
Dracula every two hours). I also really like those long-
sleeved kimono tops with hand covers. Babies are
often born with fingernails so disturbingly long it
made me wonder why nobody told me there had been
a raccoon living inside my uterus.

8. Get a bunch of the gel nipple Soothies that are free. Those are the most expensive free item at the hospital. They're the hospital equivalent of the big turkey from *Supermarket Sweep*. In fact, just steal everything from the hospital. I filled my bag with those tiny formula bottles even though I was pumping like a cow. I thought they'd come in handy for Daddy in case I happened to die from the pain and suffering of breastfeeding.

9. Take advantage of the in-house lactation consultant. Get that woman to *watch* you and correct you, because when you go home, it costs two hundred dollars to have that same exact Stevie Nicks voodoo lady come to your house and beat your engorged breast like a tambourine.

10. Take advantage of the nursery. Nurses can take care of the baby for up to three hours so you can get some sleep. Don't worry about bonding with the baby, you'll have the rest of your life to do that. Also, the baby literally can't even see. Stick that baby in the nursery, drift off, and thank me later.

11. Require all visitors to bring food from your favorite places that don't deliver. Eat sushi and deli meat, you deserve it after having been deprived of it for so long. Hell, eat food out of the trash, if you want! You are finally free to get an out-of-control listeria infection!

12. Get a blowout the day before you give birth. Once that baby comes out, sneaking in a shower where you can wash your hair is practically impossible. Plus a blowout is nice for pictures. A pedicure is also crucial before cuticle skin slowly takes over your toenails for the next three years.

13. **Make the nurses teach your partner how to change all the diapers and bathe the baby.** Remember your new mantra: *You have suffered enough.* You don't need to be changing, wiping, or teaching for a while.

14. **Bring zip-up or Velcro swaddles to the hospital.** Fuck learning how to swaddle by folding and tucking a blanket. It's not the Middle Ages. You don't need to be doing origami in the hospital.

I know this list is a lot about stealing from and taking maximum advantage of the hospital but trust me, when you go home with your partner after giving birth and realize you're all on your own, you'll thank me. Once you leave the hospital, you cannot, and hopefully will not ever, return to that mythical village of nurturing and knowledgeable women helping you squeeze water through a cheap sports bottle onto your vagina because you don't have the energy to take a shower.

CHAPTER 4

Why I Went Back to Work

Dear Girls,
    I wanted to share with you my thoughts on being a stay-at-home mom versus a working mom. Whatever path you choose, if you have children, will be the right one for you, and you don't have to commit to being either forever. I had fantasized my whole life of being a stay-at-home mom. It was my plan, my goal, my be-all-end-all. I wanted my day-to-day schedule to look like this:

Nine A.M.: Wake up and meditate.

Nine-thirty A.M.: Make and consume superfood smoothie.

Ten A.M.: SoulCycle.

Eleven A.M.: Brunch with a hypothetical black girlfriend, hypothetical Latina girlfriend, and hypothetical lesbian girlfriend (she can be whatever race she wants but she must *look* like a lesbian so that she is distinguishable from the rest of us) at a restaurant where they charge six dollars extra for an egg-whites-only omelet. We discuss bathroom remodeling, share our contractors' contact information, praise succulents for their drought tolerance, and leave a giant tip.

Two P.M.: Attend a board meeting for a foundation that gives money to organizations that build yoga studios in the hood.

Two-thirty P.M.: Nap.

Three-thirty P.M.: Meditate.

Four-thirty P.M.: Read one of Liane Moriarty's juicy novels.

Five P.M.: Gather herbs and chilies in the garden for dinner.

Six P.M.: Make dinner for Daddy.

Eight P.M.: Watch the latest HBO show that consists of maximum violence, nudity, and larger cultural conversation buzz factor.

Nine P.M.: Make love to Daddy and sleep extremely peacefully.

None of those are jokes. That's actually what I was picturing in my head. But I found out that true stay-at-home moms don't get to do any of the wonderful shit on my dream itinerary. Like, *literally* zero of those things. Because they have to be moms to *their kids,* which, strangely, I did not account for. That dream itinerary didn't even account for putting the kids to bed. I followed too many celebrities like Jessica Seinfeld on Instagram, which gave me an extremely inaccurate depiction of the stay-at-home-mom life.

I am obsessed with Jessica Seinfeld's Instagram feed. Nothing makes me more jealous, or allows me to escape the current, awful political nightmare, than her beautiful, seemingly easy life. It's 30 percent cats in bow ties, 50 percent pasta dishes she probably took two bites of, 20 percent monogrammed pillows, and 100 percent *white*. It is *unapologetically* white. God, I love it so much. Lots of time spent near water, lots of Michael Kors resort tunics, and tons of artisanal baked goods. And, though I don't really know for sure, I feel it's safe to assume she never cleans up any of the baking mess. Or any mess, really. I'd bet the only sponge she's ever seen is filled with Chantilly cream and sprinkled with edible flowers. She inserts the perfect amount of Jerry Seinfeld because I think she needs to make it clear that she's not defined by her marriage to Jerry Seinfeld while simultaneously making it clear that she's married to Jerry Seinfeld. And let's also mention that she doesn't *have* to post any of these salads or excursions to the Hamptons, because she's the wife of Jerry Seinfeld. All of this lifestyle blogging and posting is a choice, a hobby. There are no consequences if she doesn't take a picture of that fruit tart or share her thoughts on the best ballet flats. Her only real job is *to not embarrass* Jerry. And she's very good at this job because unless she were to embroider a swastika onto one of her pillows, or make cookies out of old people, everything she does is as inoffensive as one of her husband's jokes about missing socks.

Jessica Seinfeld is not a trophy wife. She is a professional socialite. A socialite is a virginal wealthy white woman who knows how to dress, behave, and decorate. The goal is to find a man like Jerry Seinfeld, a husband/sponsor/man-to-commission-whatever-creative-or-philanthropic-endeavors-you've-ever-dreamed-of-pursuing. You want to publish a cookbook? Your wish is granted! You want to start an out-reach program that provides makeup tutorials for under-privileged women? *Shazam!* But of course, as I should have known, the Instagram feeds of these kinds of women are inherently deceiving. Be careful not to be seduced by their lives because it's truly inaccessible to 99.99999 percent of us. One woman got to marry Jerry. The rest of us are stuck with Newmans.

I tried being a stay-at-home mom for eight weeks. Mari was so easy and chill, and still at the end of the day I was completely exhausted. The little things just took a lot out of me. Like, in the middle of changing her diaper, she would poo immediately onto the new diaper. Then her cute little legs would get so excited from all the expulsion and she'd kick her feet directly into the fresh poo-poo. So I'd give her a hooker bath in the sink, dry the nooks and crannies of her body to ensure no funk would form, put on her new diaper, and then minutes later . . . she'd poo again. It was a never-ending festival of feces; a real Carnival de Caca.

Mari's naps were the only time I would have to myself. People told me to nap when she napped but if I did that, when would I have time to shovel Korean instant ramen into my mouth, ask the Internet how to take care of a newborn baby, and clean up the ever growing pile of dishes and dirty clothes, stained by poo, spit, and breast milk? In one of many efforts to buy myself more time, I cut the sleeves off all of my T-shirts, leaving huge side-boob holes on each side of my shirt so that I would have quicker access to my titties to feed her. But then my nipples got so chapped from the breastfeed-ing that I just walked around topless because the friction from any fabric was too irritating, and then she'd cry and milk would automatically spray across some of our beautiful framed art on the wall, or onto our West Elm couch (which we now refer to as "the petri dish"), or it would gush down my stomach and my underwear would be soaking wet all of a sudden. The hair dryer became my best friend. I used it to dry my nipples and my tears of exhaustion.

When Daddy came home from work, I'd have a beard and be talking to a volleyball. Even though Daddy "needed time to decompress from work," I'd throw Mari into his arms and run directly into the shower. I would say things like "fuck your decompression" or through clenched teeth, "you don't know where I've been." Sometimes I'd stay in the shower for twenty minutes, just staring into space, spreading my butt cheeks with my hands so the hot water could cascade down my crack. It was the closest thing Mommy got to that hour of morning and afternoon meditation she always dreamed of.

———

I really began to rethink my plans of being a stay-at-home mom after I saw that movie *Jiro Dreams of Sushi*. It's an acclaimed documentary about the Steve Jobs of sushi in Japan. He's extremely anal about the temperature of the rice and the texture of the fish. He has two sons that are his protégés, but it's very hard for them to live up to their father's legacy. Because Jiro is so dedicated to the craft of sushi, at night he *dreams of sushi*. Everybody watched that documentary in awe of Jiro and his singular commitment to the art of fish. I watched that film and thought, *Where the fuck is Mrs. Jiro?* She isn't even *mentioned* in the goddamn documentary. Somebody had to raise those two sons while Father Jiro was busy being a sushi hero. Somebody had to wash the cum out of the sheets at night after Jiro furiously beat off to the perfect piece of glistening mackerel in his mind. What does *Mrs.*

Jiro dream of? Freedom. Recognition. Divorce. I saw that movie and decided that I wasn't gonna go out like that.

Plus, financially, I had to go back to work.

In Europe, maternity leave is amazing. New mothers get one year off, sometimes three, *paid*. In the United States, when you get pregnant, the official policy is to make you go back to work immediately, only with some plastic wrap on the floor of your cubicle to catch the afterbirth still leaking out of your pussy. It's scary in America to tell your employer that you're pregnant. On the outside, they'll generally smile and say things like "I'm so happy for you! Congrats!" But deep down, you know they're thinking, "So now you can't come in to work just because a man came inside you?! Congrats, I'm never hiring a woman ever again!"

When I got pregnant and when I gave birth to Mari, I was lucky enough to be employed at the TV show *Fresh Off the Boat*. Nahnatchka Khan, the showrunner and my boss, a fucking saint, told me to take as much time off as I needed, and that she would handle the human resources department at the studio. That's the informal maternity leave policy for any working TV writer if she has the right boss. So I still got paid my same weekly rate as a "story editor" on the show while I was busy healing from the C-section and adjusting to this new roommate (that's you, Mari!). If you ever have a boss, you need to find someone who will not snitch on you to fucking human resources when you get pregnant. If I had just been a straight stand-up comic at the time, with no other job, I never would have gotten any money during the break that I took. In stand-up comedy, you don't get paid for any shows if you're not present. I would have had to go back on the road as soon as possible to start making money for our family again.

Even if I had wanted to stay at home and not work, I really couldn't. Daddy's family made Mommy get a prenup. A "prenup" is short for a "prenuptial agreement," but what it really means is: "I *still* don't trust this bitch." So if Mommy had fallen out of the workplace completely, and Mommy and Daddy got divorced, Mommy would've been *fucked SO hard*.

My parents trained me to always picture the worst-case scenario as some sort of immigrant survival tactic. When I was in the first grade, I went to my first sleepover. As I was excitedly packing my Garfield sleeping bag and Troll dolls, my mom looked me in the eye and told me, "Make sure nobody touches your bướm [This translates to "butterfly" in Vietnamese, which is a polite way of saying "pussy."]. Nobody touches your bướm except for me when I wash you."

"Is somebody going to try to touch my bướm??"

"I don't know who is going to be at that house. A yucky uncle. A cousin. I don't know. But if you let anyone there touch your bướm you will have a very bad life. It will be traumatizing and sad and stay with you." Hey, Mom, you know what else was traumatizing and sad and stayed with me? Your terrifying warning about marauding bướm touchers!

Intent on having fun but also protecting my bướm, me and my friend took a bath together and the mom offered to wash my butt. But I pictured having "a very bad life" full of sweaty nightmares and replied confidently, "I don't wash my butt."

And then my friend told everyone at school the next day, "Ali doesn't wash her butt! Her butt smells!"

So as I signed that prenup, I imagined dedicating twenty years of my upcoming life to roasting chickens, grocery shopping, packing lunches, bedtime reading, soothing fevers, driving to soccer games, bath time, and planning, planning,

planning . . . and in doing so, becoming entirely unqualified to do stand-up. When you take more than five evenings in a row off from doing stand-up sets, you risk becoming unfunny and out of touch. And then I pictured our future children finally going off to college, and Daddy finally feeling free to leave me for his Brazilian mistress, who was so much more pleasant and younger and tighter than me, his frumpy, cranky wife whose butthole and spleen he had already memorized. And the Brazilian mistress's pussy was so good (she never had afterbirth pass through) that she was able to persuade him that I truly deserved nothing for all those years I sacrificed toward raising the children, and at the age of fifty-five, I would be back to living with an old Russian roommate in a studio apartment. No one would hire me, and they'd be right, because I actually wouldn't be qualified to do anything at all. I would have to drink Kirkland Signature baby formula to stay alive while Daddy was on a yacht, eating sashimi off his twenty-two-year-old wife's beautiful caramel ass.

I was very motivated to make my own money because I signed a document specifically outlining how much I couldn't depend on my husband. My father always praised "the gift of fear," and that prenup scared the shit out of me. In the end, being forced to sign that prenup was one of the greatest things that ever happened to me and my career.

Being a working mom is not easy and I constantly feel like I'm failing at both working and being your mom. There's never enough time to write as much as I should, or spend as much time with you two girls as I want. On my second tour, I was gone for a short three-day trip. Mari was three years old and Nikki was one. When I returned, I rushed to both of you girls, hugged you, and professed, "I missed you so much." Nikki just smiled and laughed, but Mari looked at the floor and replied angrily, "No, you didn't." It was like a knife to the heart. I felt guilty in that moment, but the truth is that I feel guilty all the time for not cooking more, for not reading more, and for not being there every single night to put each of you to bed. And I've given up on trying to be a great wife because that was kind of the point of trapping your dad with you two kids. But I feel less guilty about that.

By the time you're ready to marry, maybe there won't even be humans working anymore because of robots and you won't have to choose. Maybe in the near future, I can be a hologram comedian like Tupac at Coachella and perform in my living room for thousands of people simultaneously in Australia, Singapore, Mexico, and Mars. (Elon Musk has been trying to go there and I'd prefer he prioritize a simple speed train from San Francisco to Los Angeles, but whatever, it's his life and brain, I guess.) Either way, I know what I have in common with stay-at-home moms: We are all just doing our best. And if it isn't good enough for you, wait until you have kids and you'll get it.

CHAPTER 5

Hustle and Pho

Dear Girls,

    You can be whatever you want to be, but I'll be worried if you want to do stand-up. And because stand-up is my life's work, I have a *lot* of thoughts about it, and I'm gonna try to get them all in here.

In 2012, I went on a very sad, unofficial tour. It did not have a name because nobody even knew my name. My main TV credit was playing a best friend with no point of view or defining characteristic on a very short-lived NBC sitcom based on Chelsea Handler. I was getting paid very little to perform in these post-apocalyptic clubs, in cities where I felt like the first Vietnamese person to ever land. To save money I avoided eating out, and just ate sardines wrapped in lettuce, the meal of choice for carb-conscious hobos. On one date, I headlined the last smoking club in America. The audience looked like they had lost their way to the $3.99 Vegas buffet and decided to just sit down, to get through a pack of cigarettes before continuing their journey to unlimited pudding. I was doing stand-up in a cancer chamber. On Saturday night, I had to do three shows in a row, not because I was popular, but because the smoking-allowed policy was popular. Emphysema was a bigger draw than me. When I returned to my Travelodge room on the ground floor, right next to the freeway, I couldn't sleep on the squishy bed. My lungs felt like they'd shrunk to the size of an apple, and I was so scared someone was going to break into the room and kidnap the only Vietnamese person to ever set foot in St. Louis. I slept with my keys in between my fingers and prayed that the one time I helped an old lady cross the street would give me enough karma points to survive.

After performing nine shows over five days in that tobacco basement, I finally got to go home. I had booked the first flight out Monday morning to save money, and also because I knew I would want to go home as soon as possible. But when I arrived at the airport, the security line was serpentine, because "the system went down" (which is the adult version of "the dog ate my homework"). By the time I got to the front of the line, my flight was leaving in twenty minutes. I put my suitcase on the belt and told them I didn't want to go through the machine where you have to throw up the Jay-Z sign by making a diamond with your hands and place your feet on the yellow feet like a game of Twister. I had just spent a week performing in poison and didn't want to go through that human microwave, furthering the risk to my reproductive system and the likelihood any future baby would be born with a mouth on its elbow. When you request that, security yells out "Female Assist!" so that a pair of hands can give a five-foot-tall Chinese-Vietnamese-American struggling stand-up comedian a pat down, to check that she's not hiding a switchblade in her underwear. (Sidenote: If a small Asian woman manages to hijack a plane all by herself, she deserves to keep that plane.) Five minutes went by. Ten minutes went by. I started crying because I was missing my flight and had to be stuck in St. Louis for hours longer. Fifteen minutes. Twenty minutes. Finally, a husky and hostile woman arrived to feel me up with the backs of her hands. I stood with my arms out, legs spread, sobbing, "I just want to go home!"

The act of doing stand-up itself isn't that hard. Getting onstage in front of strangers, writing and performing jokes, and even bombing, is the *easy* part. It's everything else surrounding it that's so difficult. The road. Traveling. Spending hours on the Internet to book the cheapest flights possible. Eating a boatload of fried food with ranch dressing because there are no other options. Fending off creepy-ass men. Steering clear of your idols and funny colleagues who you've learned tend to sexually harass women.

And even at home, without the travel, it was always hard going out every night to shitty venues in shitty neighborhoods with shitty audiences and not getting paid for it. When you're starting out, stage time is so valuable. Even now, I don't get paid for a lot of sets I do locally at these bar shows, where the audience hasn't bought tickets and I'm there to test out my latest joke about my butthole. They're just there to have drinks and I'm there to workshop new material.

I get so annoyed when people claim to be stand-up comedians but they're actually comedic bloggers or vloggers. (Again, you can be whatever you want to be, but not a vlogger. Never a vlogger. Videoing yourself putting on makeup or unboxing candles is not a job.) It's really not the same. Those people don't put their *body* out there. Stand-up is extremely personal and requires you to leave your home and actually be on location. And the location is usually the back room of a Mexican restaurant in Carson. Or somebody's dog-poop-covered backyard in Silver Lake. Or an abandoned Cheesecake Factory behind an abandoned Sears.

But that's what makes it worth it.

————

Females are just as funny, if not funnier, and definitely quirkier, than men, especially in everyday life. One of your aunties (friend aunties, not blood aunties) once warmed up a frozen tamale in between her thighs at work because the microwave was broken. Another one fell asleep with her vibrator in her underwear (the batteries were dead when she found it in the morning). And another one can queef on command. I once knew a lady who would water her plants with her period juice and talk to them, hoping they'd spring to life. Good pussy jokes are funnier than good dick jokes.

But stand-up comedy is a craft that you have to hone. You have to constantly get out of the comforts of your home at night and go test out your material, at open mics, on the road. And most women don't want to do that.

Here's my personal theory on why there aren't more female stand-up comics: *safety*. When I go on the road, I have to get into a car with a stranger four times per day. From my house to the airport, from the airport to the hotel, from the hotel to the club, and from the club to the hotel. For a man that's considered an adventure, full of potential manshenanigans like in *The Hangover*. Best-case scenario is they wind up high on mushrooms getting blown by a stranger with a briefcase full of mob money and a foreign passport that doesn't belong to them. Worst-case scenario is boredom, which means being on their phones, which they also love. For a woman, though, it's four opportunities to get raped and/or killed. I got into the habit of walking at night, back to my car or to my hotel room, with keys in between my fingers, and always ready to scream and take a swipe at someone, just in case. You gotta want it really bad to constantly put yourself in those situations. You have to really love stand-up and embrace every shitty thing that comes along with it.

You also greatly increase the chances of prolonged living with your parents. Lucky for you, I'm supercool so you'll probably want to live with me. But when I started in San Francisco, living at home and being asked "Where are you going?" and "Can you pick me up from my colonoscopy?" and "Why are you doing stand-up comedy?" really ate away at my soul. I had to witness more of my parents' fights, and since I was an adult, they'd pull me into those fights. I'd be forced to listen as they aired the dirty laundry of thirty-five years of marriage, throwing out jabs at each other like: "I told you to put zero sugar in my birthday fruit tart!" and "Nobody put a gun to your head and forced you to buy ten purple polo shirts!" It was like watching a bad off-off-Broadway play where you're the only one in the audience and both the lead characters are played by your old-ass parents.

Still, San Francisco was a great place to start. I didn't know that San Francisco was a city that people moved to from all over the country specifically to start doing stand-up comedy, like my dear friend Chris Garcia (we'll talk more about him later in this chapter), who moved from L.A. The beautiful thing about starting in a city like San Francisco, Chicago, or Seattle is that you get to live in a cool, progressive metropolis, where there are smart people and interesting things happening, but you can also hide away from the entertainment industry. You don't have to worry about agents, managers, TV executives, showrunners, and casting directors watching and assessing you. A guy whose best friend is his bull piercing might be watching, but Shonda Rhimes isn't.

That's not the case in Los Angeles because you never know who is in the audience. Even now, as an established comedian, it can be exponentially more painful to test out new material in Los Angeles. When I was pregnant with Nikki, I did a last-minute pop-up show with Dave Chappelle. Opening for someone like him is always challenging because the whole energy from the crowd was: "When is Dave going up onstage?" It was at a bar on Sunset Boulevard that I had never been to before, because it looked like the kind of place where A-list celebrities go to meet and blow cocaine up one another's assholes. The lighting was very red and about one hundred people were packed into the small, intimate space. Right when I got up onstage, I noticed a man with huge black sunglasses sitting to my right, with his hood on, holding hands with a beautiful young blond model. It was Eddie Murphy. My number one comedy idol. And now the energy from the crowd wasn't: "When is Dave going up onstage?" It was: "Holy shit there's Eddie Murphy Holy shit there's Eddie Murphy who gives a shit about anything else nothing matters it's Eddie fucking Murphy!!!!" I intended to use the stage time to try out new jokes, but instead did ten minutes of my best material at the time, to complete and utter silence. And I knew Eddie Murphy specifically wasn't laughing, because everyone knows when Eddie Murphy is or isn't laughing. You could recognize his signature "HANH-HANH-HANH" goose honk anywhere. And that night, there were no geese. I couldn't believe it. I ate it so hard in front of the man who made me want to start doing stand-up comedy, and wished in that moment that I was back in San Francisco.

Nobody is great at stand-up comedy right away and it's important to have room to experiment, find your voice and, most important, to *fail*. But San Francisco was particularly special at the time when I started. It was still weird and affordable. I had barista friends renting one-bedrooms in the Mission District for five hundred dollars. The same one-bedroom would probably cost you three thousand dollars per month now and be rented out by a nineteen-year-old tech nerd who was one of the first engineers at Grubhub.

But when I was living there, San Francisco was an escape for people who hadn't been accepted in their small towns for who and what they loved or believed. This was also one of my first jokes: "There's a saying that people in New York have a lot of ambition and a lot of talent. And people in L.A. have a lot of ambition and no talent. And people who live in San Francisco go to Burning Man." It had a high density of homeless people, hippies, punks, and people who like to go to gay bars rolled up in rubber carpet so people can stand on them while they masturbate (this is a real thing, never ask me how I know). There was always this eccentric and progressive factor to it. At the Folsom Street Fair, there were men dressed up as fluorescent naughty nuns who called themselves the Sisters of Perpetual Indulgence. San Francisco was insanely liberal but, for some, it *still* wasn't enough. I remember people protesting outside Rainbow Grocery, a co-op that was known for its bulk bin selection and high number of trans employees, because it had sold cheese imported from Israel. And I'm all for standing up for what you believe in, but like, they sell organic goat curd yogurt and have a community bulletin board that's covered in spoken word fliers. They're not your enemy, liberals! The enemy is the person who told you crystal deodorant actually works.

It was healthy to start in such a sensitive and progressive environment that felt kind of oppressive, because it deserved to be mocked and people loved it. You couldn't do basic-ass trans jokes. It was a town of outsiders and we'd laugh at the insiders and also at the super outsiders who were too eccentric for the outsiders. It made sense once you understood all the Venn diagrams.

The first place I went to perform was the Brainwash Café on Folsom Street. It was run by Tony Sparks, who was known as the "Godfather of Open Mics." This is probably the worst thing to be the godfather of, after strep throat. He was an extremely charismatic man, who vaguely resembled Dr. Dre but with a giant mole and vaudevillian laugh. The Brainwash was half laundromat, half café, full homeless shelter. The comics lined up at five P.M. to sign up for a three-minute spot for an open mic showcase that would start at seven P.M. For first timers, Tony Sparks had a tradition where he announced to the audience: "Okay y'all. This here is Ali Wong. And it's her first time doing stand-up. So how about we give her—"

And the audience, composed of bitter stand-up comics, exclaimed with him, "A lot of love!"

And Tony Sparks smiled, cupping the back of his ear. "Say what?"

This time louder, everyone repeated in unison, "A lot of love!"

"I can't hear you!"

"A LOT OF LOVE!!!"

And then all the bitter comics would temporarily be awakened from their depressed-ass state, clap furiously, and scream, in awe that they were part of an actual community with actual traditions. While I did my three minutes about K-Y Jelly, and the difference between extra virgin olive oil and slutty olive oil, Tony was right there to my left, laughing and clapping. And when I got offstage, he bent down to my ear and whispered, "You gonna be famous." From that day forward, I would go up every single night at a different mic and try a million new jokes. I mostly bombed. It's the only way to get good.

One of the worst places I performed regularly at was Our Little Theater. It literally seated eight people and was located in the heart of the Tenderloin District. That neighborhood was home to Southeast Asian refugees, a million drug addicts, and a truly remarkable amount of human feces on the street. There was no time to think about my set when walking to Our Little Theater because I was too busy trying not to get robbed and jumping over doo-doo and syringes on the sidewalk. That's a game of hopscotch you *need* to win. Because if you lose, your consolation prize is ebola. Then there was the Marsh's Mock Café that had no mic stand, no stool, and no mic. There was no advertisement for the show. You had to stand outside and "bark" at strangers to please come inside, then yell your jokes at them because, again, no mic . . . at an open . . . mic.

A comic once told me to never take a stand-up comedy class because it's hacky. And it *is* hacky. If you disregard my advice and pursue stand-up, please at least do not ever take one of those courses. Doing the open-mic circuit is real stand-up comedy class. That's when you really find out if you have the strength and stamina to make a real audience laugh. The audiences for those stand-up comedy class shows are made up of friends and family of the students in the class. It's not a real audience. Those laughs aren't genuine. Those classes are a sham because they're too safe and nobody will respect you if they ever learn you took them. Again, if you become stand-ups, I'll be riddled with anxiety. But if you become stand-ups *and* take those classes, I'll say you're not my children.

Stand-up is not supposed to be warm and fuzzy or welcoming. If it was, everyone would do it. Some people think that stand-ups are all dysfunctional or have mental health problems or bad families. But I think all you need to be a good stand-up is to have a unique point of view, be funny, and enjoy bombing in front of strangers. You really do have to learn to like bombing a lot. Even now, when the audience is too good, sometimes I think, *I didn't deserve that.* You'll know you're a stand-up when, after a spectacular bomb, you don't feel like you want to quit, but instead the opposite: You want to go up again. If you don't bomb, you'll think you're good and there's no work to do. But there's always work to do. That's the beauty of stand-up. A joke is never finished. There's always more material to write. A joke can always age or get stale. It ain't music, where Mariah can sing "All I Want for Christmas" over and over. (That's my favorite song and if you don't like it, again, I'll say you're not my children.) In that sense, stand-up is a lot like fashion: It demands innovation with every new show, and you're only as good as your last collection.

Anyway, the big goal at the time was to get in at the San Francisco Punch Line to get a hosting gig. But when you host, you have to go up first, in front of a cold audience that isn't there to see you and is getting served drinks while you're doing your best to fluff them. They haven't had any alcohol yet. I hated hosting so hard and am *so* relieved to not have to do it anymore. I missed my oldest sister's bachelorette party, which was a small getaway in Napa, to host for a semi-high-profile headliner at a club in Sacramento. At the time, he was in his seventies and I was so excited to meet him and work with him that week. I left San Francisco at three-thirty P.M., drove in rush hour Friday traffic and arrived at the club at seven P.M. for an eight P.M. show start. I waited and waited and his feature act assured me that he would show up by eight forty-five P.M. He arrived five minutes before his headlining set at eight-forty P.M. and I enthusiastically greeted him: "Hi! I'm Ali. I'm the host for this week. Is there anything you want me to say in particular for your intro?" He didn't answer me; he didn't even look at me. He just walked past me into the green room and closed the door, which I took as a clear message that I was never to step in there again for the entire week. Still, after reminding the crowd to tip the bar and waitstaff, I gave the man a glowing intro with all of his TV credits, and talked about how much I looked up to him. Usually when I introduce somebody to an audience, there's some sort of handshake or hug, a physical exchange between me and the person that is about to go up, to offer a connecting piece between me and the next performer. But again, he just walked past me like I wasn't there. Too scared to go into the green room, I just hung outside of the club kitchen, sitting on a metal fold-out chair, where the smell of frozen chicken tenders and buffalo sauce enveloped me. I sat there laughing at his set, but also disappointed that some of his references were really old and obscure. El DeBarge and Macarena jokes don't belong anywhere past the year 1998. At the second ten-thirty P.M. show, his feature opener left five minutes after he got offstage. "Where are you going?" I asked.

"To my hotel to sleep," he responded. "Get ready to be here for a while."

I wish he would've told me that "a while" meant until one-thirty A.M. As the host, you have to stay until the very end of the show to bookend it. Just to tell everyone good night and make whatever announcements the club needs you to make. My ass hurt from sitting on that metal chair and mostly I was concerned about the two-and-a-half-hour drive back home to San Francisco. Despite drinking two cups of coffee, my head was bobbing in and out of a sleepy state while I was driving my 1989 Volvo sedan on the freeway, blasting Tupac's "California Love" to keep me awake. And on Saturday, I drove back to Sacramento and did it all over again. That week we did a total of four shows together and not once did he ever make eye contact with me. Maybe you wanted some sort of #MeToo story about hosting. But someone doesn't have to grab your ass for him to be an asshole.

Sunday was the local stand-up comedy showcase at the San Francisco Punch Line Comedy Club. At the time, Kevin Avery, Joe Klocek, or W. Kamau Bell would always close the show. A handful of other San Francisco comedy veterans who had been living there for over a decade were all guaranteed a spot. A lot of them were in their forties and extremely bitter. Some of them had tried to move to L.A. and failed. Some of them never even tried. There were only thirteen spots on that Sunday showcase and up to sixty comics watching and waiting from the back, at the bar, hoping to get one of those spots. The booker, Molly Schminke, a beautiful majestic tattooed red-headed mermaid, would somehow keep track of all the comics and how long and how consistently they had been waiting. Often people had to sit back there for a year and a half before getting their first spot/audition on the Sunday showcase. When I finally went up, when I finally got my chance after months of waiting . . . I ate it. I was so nervous and had worked so hard on that seven-minute set but it was met with utter silence and awkward stares. I bombed so bad that other comics didn't want to talk to me or look me in the eye afterward because they didn't want to have to acknowledge the tragedy that had just passed onstage. That's when you know you really died up there: when other comics treat you like you just farted. But I kept coming every Sunday.

Molly gave me another shot three months later, and I killed. Then she had me host the Sunday showcase three months after that, and I got my first hosting gig with Rex Navarrete. Eventually I got to host for Dave Chappelle, Dave Attell, Doug Benson, Marc Maron, Patrice O'Neal, and Janeane Garofalo, all of whom helped me later on in life.

But the Punch Line did not offer enough stage time with the Sunday showcase and twice-per-year hosting gigs, so I would go to the alternative rooms to grow. These were monthly shows people would put on at bookstores, restaurants, community centers, and rock clubs. With the skills I learned from LCC, an Asian American student theater group I joined at UCLA, I produced and promoted my own shows right away. Some of my favorite stand-up comedy show titles were *Hustle and Pho, The Cameltoe Show,* and *Jungle Beaver.* It was the only way I could headline and do an hour of material, since I was limited to five minutes at the open mics, fifteen minutes hosting the Punch Line, and twenty minutes max at other people's alternative shows. I was very dirty back then. Even now I'll look back on those days and think, *God, you were* disgusting. I would talk about having to waddle to the toilet, with my hand cupped below my pussy to catch cum drippings after sex. I'd also put my foot up on the stool and mime splashing water on my vagina in a sink, to get rid of the dried pussy flakes, right before having sex.

Chris Garcia and I started a stand-up and sketch variety show called *Rice and Beans.*

One night, after a year of solid friendship, it was my birthday, and we went out and got extremely drunk at a club on Haight Street. When we were getting ready to call it a night, he ran into the middle of traffic and started waving his penis around. My friend Vanessa said it was like a very primal mating call. And then in the back of Vanessa's Volvo sedan (this was a very popular car at the time in the Bay Area, before Subaru took over with their chic lesbian appeal), we started to make out. I threw up all over him, and then we kept making out.

We got into a relationship right away. It was the first time I ever had a serious boyfriend who wasn't Asian American. Chris was Cuban American, a party dog, and *very* funny. We decided to keep our relationship a secret to avoid people treating us differently (this is a weird high school thing to do, but the SF comedy scene was high school part two). People would ask if we were dating and he'd respond: "No way, dude, she looks like a Monchhichi doll. Anne Geddes babies are not my thing." I loved to write jokes with him at this tiny table at the Brainwash Café. We'd sit there in the corner, roasting all of the eccentric people coming and going. There was one comic who had long hair in front of his face and as he went up onstage, Chris said to me, "Oh, I didn't recognize Slash without the guitar." At our *Rice and Beans* sketch show, we performed another sketch called "American Apparel" where we both wore tight unitards, wristbands, tube socks, and headbands and would dance to bad techno SoulCycle instrumentals while whispering "American Apparel" over and over again. Chris bent over in front of the audience and let one of his balls pop out. Again, him and those primal mating calls. We were just young and dumb.

But things started to fall apart eventually. I got frustrated because, like many men I had been drawn to before, he did some irresponsible-ass shit that made me feel like his mom. He borrowed my sister's car and it got towed twice in San Jose because he didn't read the damn parking signs. When we broke up, he said to me, "Look, we're just different, okay? You like to save money and take care of your body. I like to go to the mall and eat hot dogs." That is ultimately not a flattering thing to say about yourself but it was so honest and makes us both laugh to this day. It took a long time, but now Chris and I are friends. He was my only stand-up comedy friend who came to my father's funeral. Years later, when he had gotten married and I was already married and had Mari, I made sure to attend his father's funeral as well. In tears from Chris's moving eulogy, I approached his mother and asked, "Me recuerdes?" (Remember me?)

She shook her head.

"Soy la novia Chinita que encanto su arroz con pollo." (I'm the small Chinese girlfriend who loved your chicken with rice.)

"Ohhhhhh!!!!!" She laughed, through tears, and squeezed my arm. "Gracias por venir." (Thank you for coming.)

———

As much as I would love having you girls live near me, you will thrive if you move somewhere else. At some point you gotta go. Mama loves you but it's so important to get out of your hometown and get the fuck away from your family. As the youngest of four kids, I was always being observed by my siblings, who would judge my every decision. They had a set idea of who I was and it affected me. It was limiting. Everything I said generally had no credence because I was at least

ten years younger than every single person in my family, so
what did I really know? When I got away from them, I finally
felt like I could be the person I was meant to be, which just
happened to be a person who talked about her wish to put
nail polish remover in men's buttholes so she could accom-
plish two things at once. Chances are that neither of you is
also that person.

My family had always told me how to speak and how to
feel about things. Part of what was so liberating about being
onstage was that I could say whatever I wanted without having loved ones comment on it. Regardless of how the strangers would respond, at least they were strangers who didn't
know me or have any real authority over who I was. I loved
the anonymity of my conversations with an audience.

But deciding to move to NYC after four years of doing
stand-up in San Francisco was hard. Before I packed up, my
best friend told me how her friend had witnessed a rat giving
birth on a homeless lady's lap on the subway. And that single
image pretty much sums up New York. I lived in a loft with
eight other people, including that sixty-seven-year-old Russian lady. I temporarily filled in as the receptionist at a cleft
palate surgery non-profit.

I was twenty-six at the time, and there were girls who were
just out of college ordering me around. They had much nicer
bags and shoes than I did. I remember admiring this one
program director's bag, and thought I could afford it since it
was nylon. She was horrified that I wasn't already familiar
with the "Longchamp Le Pliage" bag and told me it was a
"staple" in every woman's closet. I immediately looked it up
online and saw that it cost over a hundred dollars. *For a nylon
bag*. I thought, *Bitch, I could eat twenty-five Mamoun's falafel
sandwiches for that bag*.

Every day in NYC was about spending as little money as possible. I didn't see any movies or eat out unless I went out on a date, or it was pizza or falafel. Ninety percent of the time I cooked at the SoHo loft. I'd buy lentils from a bulk bin at an East Village co-op and boil them to eat with salt, like a medieval peasant. And then I'd steam some vegetables from Chinatown. For three dollars and fifty cents, I found a place that sold half of a cooked chicken that was probably loaded with enough antibiotics to turn my blood into Purell.

NYC is and was cartoonishly expensive. Once, in the middle of the night, I got my period and was very unprepared. I had no choice but to walk to the local bodega in SoHo to load up on all the necessary gear. Midol and tampons cost me fifteen dollars (that's a lot). There was no beloved Costco or Target to rely on. Instead, I was forced to "support a local business," and that business returned the favor by price gouging the shit out of me. I could've put a down payment on one of those overpriced French nylon bags for all the money I spent that evening.

Friends and family kept asking me how I was doing in NYC and I just didn't know what to tell them. They were wondering, "So have you MADE IT YET??!!" And no, I never really made it in New York. But in retrospect, the loneliness was good for me. It caused me to focus. There were nights where I would perform nine sets in one evening because that was the whole purpose of me moving to NYC, but also there was nothing else for me to do.

Years later, I returned to New York to play an agoraphobic radiologist on an ABC medical drama called *Black Box*. I was so excited to finally have money in New York and literally screamed, "Started from the bottom, now we here!" as I got off the plane. I arrived at my West Village apartment, said hi to my two other roommates, started sweating trying to squeeze my suitcases into my tiny-ass bedroom, and then whispered to myself, "Oh fuck, I'm still at the bottom." That apartment was the best I could afford. The shower was the size of an RV shower, and the water turned from cold to hot, hot to cold very fast, which I'm pretty sure is the same technique they used to torture prisoners in Guantánamo Bay. I would have to do breathing exercises before getting in that telephone booth of water hell.

———

As a female comic, it was always hard to not date a stand-up comedian. Mostly because when I dated men outside of stand-up comedy, their *attempts* at funny made me cringe. One guy pointed to an escalator that was out of order and said to me, "Escalators that are out of order are basically temporary stairs." I said to him, "That's a Mitch Hedberg joke." He said to me, "Oh, I just came up with that thought on my own by myself." Shut up, you fucking liar. One Filipino guy said to me, "I'm not a Jew, I'm Jew-ISH." It made no sense because, first of all, he was a Filipino Catholic and not even part Jewish. Second of all, that was another old joke stolen from a real comedian.

Then a white guy tried to neg me after a show and said, "Hey, are you Asian, or do you just look sleepy?" First of all, so racist and rude. Second of all, that's a racist and rude *Don Rickles* joke, you dickhead.

Male friends of your father have told me that it makes them uncomfortable that I'm professionally funny. They get angry at me for not laughing at their dumb stories about their wives. "She makes a fuss when I put all my stuff in her purse and I'm like, look how many shoes you put into my closet! Hahahahahahaha!" At a wedding, one of them came up to me and said, "Hey, Ali, my wife is so bossy, she always gets on my case for not putting the toilet seat down. I'll put down the toilet seat once you put down that *People* magazine!" I just want to shake these men by the shoulders and say, "You will never be funnier than me and that's *okay*. Don't worry, you still have a bigger dick than me!"

Pretty much the worst thing about being a woman in stand-up is that you are always forced to socialize with male stand-up comics' girlfriends. You become a babysitter for these poor women. At a club once, this comic dumped his life-sized Barbie doll of a girlfriend next to me, like, *Hey, can you watch this?* To be fair, she was perfectly nice and was showing me all of the fancy stuff on her body that her boyfriend had bought her. "I mean, just look at this diamond. It's a honey diamond, which I think is a very chic alternative to a basic diamond. Honey because it's the color of honey!" she exclaimed as she searched for light to rotate her wrist in, to maximize the sparkle on her finger. "Look at my Casio digital watch," I replied as I offered my wrist to her hands. "It cost $19.99, and it displays the time AND date!" She didn't get the sarcasm and instead pretended to just be super impressed. "Oh my God! That's really um . . . useful and such a neat retro watch! You're like one of those kids riding a bike in *E.T.*!" Again, she was perfectly nice but it was grueling talking to someone who didn't understand sarcasm.

Another time this mousy girl was plopped down next to me at the Comedy Cellar by a brilliant comic twenty-five years her senior. She told me proudly, "I'm a humorist!"

"Oh," I said, "like David Sedaris. I love David Sedaris."

She rolled her eyes. "No, not like David Sedaris. He is so mainstream now."

"Yeah," I responded sarcastically. "He's basically a McDonald's hamburger, that David Sedaris."

"Exactly."

I wish I could say I stopped talking to her but if you think like a woman, you're scared of being a bitch, and it was much more terrifying for all of us before Cersei Lannister in *Game of Thrones* made it cool.

I just stared at that comic's girlfriend and kept my mouth full of hummus and pita so I'd have an excuse not to respond.

The dudes want to be free to socialize with their friends, so I become girlfriend daycare. A lot of those girls get seduced by the man's ability to be funny, and then get pissed a couple months later when they realize he doesn't have any money. What I sometimes say to them from the get-go is:

"Baby girl, I'm his actual friend and *even I* don't believe in him. Move to Silicon Valley, find yourself a nice engineer."

Comedy Girlfriend: "But engineers aren't funny."

Me: "Trust me, if you lived in a mansion, you'd be laughing *all the time.*"

The absolute worst is when one of those women is an aspiring stand-up comic and expects me to help her skip the line. I'm down to help people out if I can, but only *after they've paid their dues.* And I'm not one of those women who doesn't like other women. I *love* women. They always bring snacks and smell nice and read fiction and enjoy hot beverages and sitting down while eating and, like I said, are way funnier than men. I get overly excited when I get to see any of my fellow female stand-ups—we go into a corner and just talk shit about other comics, trade tips on how to best handle the road, and lately they all ask me about how I make motherhood and stand-up work. I'm happy to share and now that some of them, like Natasha Leggero, Amy Schumer,

Chelsea Peretti, Christina Pazsitzky, and Sabrina Jalees, are mothers, I cannot wait to see them more.

I generally hate the question "What is it like to be a female comedian?" because it suggests females aren't supposed to be funny, and that it's news when we are funny. Of course I ultimately understand the question, because the biggest challenge in stand-up for me was the opening joke. I always had great closers, and I knew I was funny, but convincing an audience that a person who looks like me could be funny, and proving to them that I belonged onstage, was a steep uphill battle. Larry David looks like he's supposed to be funny. Richard Pryor, Dave Chappelle, Louie Anderson . . . all look funny. There's precedent for someone who looks like them to be telling jokes.

Once while performing in Honolulu in my early twenties, I got up onstage and literally heard a man say, "Oh no, this is gonna suck." He was sitting in the front row with his blond hair, blue eyes, and three Greek letters on his tank. He looked like he was born on a ski slope and bred to commit white-collar crime to perfection. His three friends, who I assume were named Brett, Chet, and Thor, sighed and rolled their eyes in agreement with their arms folded. But as my set progressed, and climaxed with me pulling down my pants and showing my butt crack, they were slapping the table and pushing one another's biceps while howling in laughter. The leader who was initially very mean bought a T-shirt from me after the show. It was an American Apparel women's medium, because that was the only size left, but he took off his fraternity tank, squeezed his new Ali Wong shirt with Ali Wong's face on it over his giant block of a head, and high-fived me as the shirt rose above his belly button like a sports bra. "You are AWESOME!" he exclaimed as he walked away with the rest of the eighties teen villains who had decided the nerds weren't that bad after all.

I felt a need to utterly de-sexualize myself for the stage and the whole scene of stand-up comedy. When I first started, I would wear my hair up in two buns that made me look like Mickey Mouse and dress myself in huge cargo pants (I worshipped Aaliyah because she was like a sexy female minotaur with her sparkly bra on top and tomboy pants on the bottom) and a skater shirt. Somehow I thought the audience would take me seriously the more I looked like Sailor Moon's butch friend. But I started wearing my hair down when I finally felt more secure that I was going to make the audience laugh no matter what I looked like.

There are too many niche stand-up shows these days. I see a lot of Asian-themed stand-up comedy shows that feature an all–Asian American lineup, and while I love that it provides more stage time for comics just starting out, it can quickly become a crutch. I remember a Filipino guy when I was starting out who would only perform on the Asian American stand-up circuit, which was super small. He'd joke about lumpia and Daly City and debuts (Filipino quinceañeras and bar mitzvahs) and Manny Pacquiao. He was very funny, but it was almost impossible for anyone who wasn't Filipino and from the Bay Area to understand his jokes. He admitted to me that he became scared to perform in front of any other audience. Last I heard, he doesn't do stand-up anymore.

Comedy requires taking risks. Performing in front of an audience that's not your crowd is huge. When I went to Atlanta for the first time three years into stand-up comedy, I performed all around the city in front of all-black audiences. One night, I followed this guy in a wheelchair who killed so fucking hard that the room was shaking. He danced for the first three minutes of his set and talked about how his dick still works for the next two. I watched from the side, not even registering the last five minutes of his set because I was so nervous about going after him. People in the audience were jumping up and down, screaming in support of this charismatic guy who was delivering an extremely funny and bizarrely uplifting set.

Then the host, a local radio personality with a big white beard, bald head, and diamond earrings, introduced me in his raspy voice by saying, "You know this next comedian. She does your nails. She does your laundry. Please welcome to the stage Ah-li Wang!" In my Adidas black-and-red track jacket and baggy cargo pants, I went up there completely in shock of his terrible introduction. A good intro is supposed to build you up, to make you larger than life. Instead, this one reduced me down to two of the most basic stereotypes. And he got my name wrong. When I got to the microphone, my voice was shaking and I started talking about mixing up the K-Y Jelly with the toothpaste. Soon, I heard a couple of people yelling "boo!" like the first couple drops of rain. Then they just multiplied and multiplied until I was chased offstage by a hurricane of boos. I couldn't have been onstage longer than three minutes before I quit. I almost felt like never performing again, period. But then I realized that for the past three years, I had been performing in San Francisco, in front of mostly white and Asian people, and that I needed to get out of that.

So from then on, I diversified my crowds. I performed in Oakland a lot more, and said yes to every opportunity possible to do a set in other cities, even if it meant losing money. I think a lot of young comics now get too comfortable at these small, niche shows where everybody looks and thinks like them, and nobody is paying real money, so the audience is there just to be seen and feel the fervor of being surrounded by like-minded people. It's like they all came out to see a performance of "Social Media Echo Chamber: Live!" I see so many young comics with lots of promise, but their sets are not tight. Learning how to get as many laughs as possible per minute is a skill born out of necessity. And thinking that a crowd of strangers wants to hear your sad story or enlightened political ideas at a comedy show without consistent laughs throughout is a bad habit born out of entitlement. Save the speech for a TED talk or brunch.

———

The question "What should I wear?" has always been tougher for female stand-ups. I see some men just wearing zip-up hoodies in their HBO or Netflix specials, which is smart, because that's what they're comfortable in, what they're *used to* performing in. It's always a little odd when I see a fellow female stand-up comic friend performing in a wildly uncomfortable sexy dress with a side zip and heels. None of us (except for the great Natasha Leggero who puts on an Oscar De La Renta evening gown to get the mail) wears that when we're performing locally, doing sets at the Comedy Cellar in NYC or at the Comedy Store in Los Angeles. We're usually wearing sneakers, T-shirts, jeans and, in my case, a pantyliner. I never feel safe and confident if I don't have a pantyliner in my underwear.

If either of you ever decide to do stand-up (for the last time, please don't) and do a special or any sort of taping, always perform in flats. There's an old Chinese proverb that goes, "You die from the feet up." Our feet are crucial toward our movement and health, and inform your every step onstage. You girls will inevitably go through a phase where you want to wear heels. My old pal Beyoncé does it magically. But please remember that your performance should never be limited by your shoes. It's not worth your calves looking 20 percent better.

My very first late-night set was on *The Tonight Show*, and I wore this bright pink dress with three-inch heels. I was so excited to occupy the airwaves for five minutes straight and wanted to look good while doing it. All I could think about for days leading up to the TV appearance was how I was going to be able to manage talking without seeming like I was constipated. I dreaded wearing those heels so much that I didn't even practice my set in them when warming up for it around Los Angeles. My five-minute takeover of NBC ended up being pretty mediocre. My delivery came off as stiff, and I rushed through the whole thing. Somehow vanity got in the way again for my second late-night set, which was on Seth Meyers. I wore skinny jeans that fit perfectly into black boots with three-inch heels. At the time, I thought the ankle support would make a big difference. It made zero. Once again, I was mentally occupied with how my body was going to handle all of these things I put on it and, as a result, came off like a sedated circus bear on camera. Around town, I had always performed in sneakers or sandals. Stand-up is not about being pretty or looking your best, it's about being yourself and being funny, period. You can always look pretty in a picture or at a party later.

———

The most I ever felt like a real outsider as a female comedian was when I got pregnant the second time. A hacky comic came up to me, touched my belly without asking my permission with his chubby hand and molester mustache, and said, "So this is your hook, this is your thing, right?"

"Getting pregnant is not rainbow suspenders. It is also not a sustainable career strategy. Do you expect me to get pregnant eight times?"

"You know what I mean. You're so lucky, Ali. Me, I'm just another white guy. But you are both a female *and* a minority," he said.

Yes, because historically that has always been the winning combo for recognition and success in the entertainment industry. First of all, it's not okay to touch a woman's pregnant belly without asking. My belly is still my body that has another body inside of it, neither of which belongs to you. So please back the fuck up. I didn't even know the last name of this comic or if his parents were still alive, yet he felt like it was perfectly acceptable to lay his sweaty, hairy flesh on a very sacred part of my body. Why don't you just go ahead and finger me while you're at it? What that guy should've said to me was "Congratulations." It's really not that complicated, dude.

In the world of stand-up comedy, I've felt an increasing amount of jealousy and resentment from certain white male comics for being a woman of color. I hear that line a lot: *Me, I'm just another white guy.* Here's a solution: Try being a funnier white guy. There are plenty of white guys out there, like Jimmy Kimmel, John Mulaney, Nick Kroll, Bill Hader, Sebastian Maniscalco, Joe Rogan, Jimmy Fallon, Stephen Colbert, James Corden, Neal Brennan, Jeff Ross, Moshe Kasher, John Cena, Ike Barinholtz, Judd Apatow, Seth Rogen, Chris D'Elia, Dave Attell, Jeff Ross, Brian Regan, Ron White, Marc Maron, Jerry Seinfeld, Ricky Gervais, Conan O'Brien, Jim Gaffigan, Jeff Dunham, Patton Oswalt, Steve Martin, Bill

Burr, Steven Wright, Jon Stewart, David Letterman, John Oliver, Ben Stiller, Bo Burnham, Mike Myers, and Will Ferrell, to name thirty-eight out of eight million, who all seem to be doing just fine.

I get so annoyed at those resentful men for reducing any of my success to attention for being a woman, being Asian, or being pregnant. I struggled and hustled for so long. Plus, going on the road pregnant was not easy. During the first trimester, I was insanely tired because my body was busy hosting this growing guest. I would fall asleep every time my butt hit a couch. I remember my head feeling so heavy all the time, like if I didn't get into a horizontal position soon, it was gonna snap off my neck. I got nauseous through my second trimester. On a plane ride to Boston, Daddy didn't brush his teeth well enough. His breath smelled like a dirty diaper and he'd just watched the movie *Selma* and couldn't stop talking about it. I kept telling him to back up, but he wouldn't, and I threw up immediately into a red Lululemon shopping bag that had all of these inspirational quotes on the outside like "Dance as if nobody is watching." Actually, I threw up in several Lululemon bags while I was pregnant. They are very sturdy and make incredible lunch bags for the plane. And those quotes made me feel like it was okay to ralph like nobody was watching.

Going on the road as a woman has always felt dangerous, scary, and lonely. Now as a mom traveling with my family, it's none of those three things. But it is a fucking hassle. I'm writing all the jokes, packing two huge suitcases, lugging the car seat and stroller, going through security, getting on a plane at five A.M., posting announcements for these shows on Instagram and Twitter, performing two shows back-to-back, not being able to sleep in during the day or save my voice because

I have to take care of my kids whose sleep schedules are all fucked up because we're in a new time zone.

And even when we don't fly, it's rough. I was on my way to a San Diego show in Friday afternoon traffic from Los Angeles. Mari and Grandma were in the car with me. I was in gridlock traffic and there was no end in sight. I was driving and had to pee *so bad*. I finally told Grandma, "Grab me one of Mari's diapers." It was a size 3 diaper, so it was designed to hold the pee of a human under twenty pounds. I shoved the diaper in my underwear, pressed it against my pussy, and peed into it. The diaper filled up within two seconds. Then I told Grandma to grab me another diaper. And another. And another. Mari, I peed into five of your diapers and felt a huge sense of victory. "Pimp of the Year" by Dru Down happened to start playing on the radio. I threw up my arms (it's okay, like I said, I was stuck in traffic so it was perfectly safe to take my hands off the steering wheel to celebrate) and screamed "Woooooo!" while my mom was laughing. I had hacked this problem. I was "the Wolf" from *Pulp Fiction*. I finally understood what they meant by *having it all*. Three generations of women in one car together, making family and career work. Then I realized there was pee dripping down my legs and pooling in the seat of my brand-new RAV4 (a situation they never show you how to handle in the commercials). So maybe I guess you *can't* have it all? If I were a man and had a penis, I could've just pissed into my Swell water bottle. (Actually, I have yet to see a man with a Swell water bottle. Make that a Big Gulp cup.)

But without the both of you, I would have nobody to write this book to. I also wouldn't have ever gotten a book deal. So if you *must* do stand-up comedy, please always have someone walk you back to your car. Mama will go with you

and carry a hockey stick or a metal club to protect you—
I mean, what else am I going to do in retirement? Garden?
We turned our entire backyard into Astroturf because I
learned plants bring bugs and spiders, and spiders bring certain death. I've let succulents die. Succulents are the Volvos
of plants. As indestructible as they are unsexy. I tried knitting
and gave up when I realized how much more fun it is to buy
a sweater at Target for ten dollars. And I'm definitely not
going to take classes when I retire. What is the point of learning how to speak French like a second-grader when you're
gonna die so soon? "Où est le cemetery? Je suis une old-ass
person who shouldn't be learning a new damn language!"

But when I'm not around to walk with you back to your
car, lace your keys in between your fingers like I did in that
motel. If some headliner is using his power and status to do
some creepo shit, scream and leave. Tell everyone. Take a
picture of his crooked dick and tweet that shit immediately. I
don't care how funny or beloved someone is. Take his ass
down if he fucks with you. Don't let anyone pressure you into
hooking up for fear that if you don't fuck them, he'll be angry
and blackball you.

Just tweet his dick, trust me.

CHAPTER 6

Snake Heart

Dear Girls,
        I highly encourage you to study abroad at some
point. In fact, I'm just going to make you do it. If you don't,
I swear I will burn all of my limited edition tracksuits that I
know you guys will want when you're big enough to fit them.

Bottom line: Spending a significant amount of time outside the United States in your formative years makes you a
better person. You learn things from simply living your day-
to-day life in another country that can't be taught in a classroom, like open-mindedness and empathy. Plus, you get to
eat delicious food and (hopefully) fuck hot foreigners. My
junior year at UCLA, I did study abroad in Hanoi, Vietnam.
But the summer before, I did a program at the University of
Hawai'i via UCLA for two months to study Native Hawaiian
Sovereignty. It's not technically going abroad since Hawai'i is
one of the fifty states. (Which a lot of the people on my pro-

gram didn't seem to understand. In fact, there was a girl who also thought you could run from one end of the island to the other.) But it still gave me valuable perspective on how people live in different places. Plus it was Hawai'i! I was expecting to have this great summer where I'd hang out in my bikini and drink piña coladas while a bunch of local surfers of mixed Asian-American-Hawaiian-Portuguese descent would take turns licking my taint.

But instead, the program was 98 percent women. The three boys on it were Friend-Zone material (that's the nicest way I know how to say they were ugly). So it turned into this power women–bonding experience where we all ate Spam musubi every day from the local 7-Eleven and drank Olde English forties every night. None of us got any ass because we were too busy inhaling kalua pig, white rice, and haupia and getting gassy from overeating. Somewhere in my closet, there's a pile of pictures of us singing karaoke with puke on our shirts. My three roommates and I threw up and shat so much into our one toilet that the seat broke after two weeks. And instead of fixing it, we chose to just hover over the seatless toilet bowl for the rest of the program. That hovering was also the most exercise we got the whole time.

You might be wondering how eating, drinking, shitting, and puking so much could be considered a "valuable experience," but being around all of those women on the program, with no men to impress, was so empowering. We were as boisterous as we wanted to be, without having to worry it would be too much for any man to handle, and we were having fun for ourselves. And it was from that summer on that I decided I should just live with this attitude forever, regardless if there were men around or not.

One of my roommates was Citadelle Bliss Priagula. Filipinos straight up have the best names. Here's a fun formula for working out your Filipino name: *Favorite type of candle* + *Favorite brand of body wash* + *Name of a dragon in* Game of Thrones = *your Filipino name*. Mine is Citronella Dove Viserion.

Citadelle and I would stay up late talking ourselves to sleep. One night, we decided to have an epic staring contest. In our spaghetti strap nightgowns, we sat across from each other on our cheap twin dorm beds, with our eyes wide open. She tried flaring her nostrils and I was like, *Bitch, please*. I finally got her by inhaling deeply and then shooting snot out of my nose onto my lips. When in doubt, use your own bodily fluids to destroy your enemy. Your body is a well-stocked arsenal of goos and liquids—don't be afraid to use it.

I gained ten pounds and it was the best summer of my life. The curriculum was so interesting and I was very fortunate to hear the great Haunani-Kay Trask speak passionately about her people's right to get back their land, and how ready she was for the exploitation of Native Hawaiians via the tourism industry to stop. At the end of her speech, a fellow student raised her hand to ask: "My family is Japanese American and has been in Hawai'i for many generations. What can we do to support the sovereignty movement? What can we do to help?"

And Haunani-Kay Trask simply responded: "Get out." And then she followed up by proudly and unapologetically stating: "I have zero aloha. None."

The way she used humor and spoke with such strength, all while in her sarong and long hair flowing down to her elbows, really inspired me and influenced how I perform. I loved how she didn't try to repress her beauty or femininity in order to appear more authoritative. In fact, she channeled it into this goddess-queen energy that made her come off as a captivating maternal figure fighting for her beliefs and her people. I had never been so moved by a single speaker.

Then I gained five more pounds because fuck it.

―――――

After that summer in Hawai'i, I went to Vietnam and gained ten *more* pounds. Clothing store employees wouldn't even let me try on anything in their shops. I walked into one store to find some new clothes, and the young girl aggressively yanked a pair of pants out of my hands and said in broken English, "This: small. You: bigger."

I gained weight for a number of reasons. The food was so good and basically free, so I would eat even when I wasn't hungry. Back then, a bowl of pho was fifteen cents. *Fifteen cents*. Nothing is that cheap. A pack of gum doesn't even come close. I once ordered a side of anchovies at a famous pizza place in New York and they charged me ten dollars. Ten dollars for *anchovies,* the pigeons of the sea!

It blew my mind how far the U.S. dollar could go; it felt like the entire country was on sale. And like my cheap uncle says, the best thing about Vietnam: "NO TIP." No wonder why gross, loser American men love to go to Southeast Asia to feel powerful. "I'm an expat" is a very fancy way for these men to say "No one would fuck me in America" and "I'm a pervert who wants to sleep with as many Asian women as possible." One of those guys once mistook me for a native Vietnamese woman and kept trying to seduce me in Vietnamese. He had a huge red beard, John Lennon glasses, and looked like he had spent his whole life eating and smelling like Fritos while writing a fantasy novel that he would never finish about queens and dragons. Over and over, he repeated

"Chị ơi!" (which means "Hey lady!") from a balcony as I shopped on the street. I wish I had screamed up at him, "Go away! I'm from the United States! You ain't locking me in no expat sex dungeon!" But instead I just walked away as fast as possible, hoping he wouldn't throw a fishing net on me and then drag me up into his spider's nest of red pubes and SPF40.

It was so much fun to eat on the street, on a red plastic stool at a tiny table. I could tell myself whatever meal I ate didn't really count since I was eating in a dollhouse. I couldn't resist all the street vendors. I loved flagging down a woman riding a bicycle, with steaming orange, yellow, and green sticky rice on display behind her. And she'd repeat in a sing-song tone what she was selling like a seductive siren from Greek mythology: "HOT STICKY SWEET RICE HOT STICKY SWEET RICE HOT STICKY SWEET RICE." By the third announcement I'd be making it rain, begging her to wrap that rice in newspaper, sprinkle it with coconut shavings, and *please* give it to me already. I loved having a relationship with the people who made my food, and how low stakes it was to try new things.

Those street vendors were so ephemeral, like an occult gift shop that vanishes after selling you a cursed monkey's paw. One of my favorite things to eat in the morning was soft tofu with caramelized ginger syrup. This woman would come around on her bike every morning in front of my house and sell me some. Then one day, she stopped coming and I heard she died. It was so traumatizing that from then on, I decided to eat every one of my favorite food items from my favorite food vendors, even if I was full. I was acting like a survivor in a post-apocalyptic zombie world who stumbles on a supermarket.

Writing about this is making me insanely hungry. It's a miracle I was able to even get an education while being so focused on eating. Sorry to go on, but what I always miss about Vietnamese food from Vietnam is the wide diversity of noodle soups. Pho is kind of like the pad thai of Vietnamese food. It became the most desirable and commercial Vietnamese dish for mainstream America, because there's nothing too scary about it. It wasn't until I lived in Vietnam that I realized about thirty different kinds of noodle soups were far superior to pho. One of my favorites was miến lươn, which is essentially clear noodles with fried eels in a very tasty pork-based clear broth. This one vendor would set up shop on the same corner near my house every day at five P.M. I'd watch her walk to the corner, balancing one large pot of broth on one end of a bamboo stick, with another pot full of noodles, dishes, herbs, and eels. Whenever I went more than three days without eating at her stand, she'd ask me why and where I had been, like a jealous wife. All of the vendors just sold one thing. They didn't diversify their menu to risk lowering the quality of the one dish they did really well. They were on the opposite of the Cheesecake Factory menu model where you can order a General Tso's chicken with a side of borscht.

Every morning I ate trứng vịt lộn, also known as balut. It's a fertilized duck embryo, served piping hot and, for your average American, *Fear Factor* food. It was tough to look at, I admit. The brown baby bird is full of visible veins and has feathers and a tiny beak. But I was sitting next to five-year-old kids on their way to school, and they were eating it, so I thought, *Fuck it, if these first-graders can handle the feathers, so can I.* I tried my best to watch and copy them as they confidently struck the eggshell and immediately sucked the dark juice out of the opening. I was shocked at how delicious it was, how it tasted like a very concentrated chicken broth. And the yolk was so dense, buttery, and perfect when paired with this spicy green herb and a little bit of salt. I had been hesitant to eat it because it was the epitome of unprocessed food. It was practically still alive, but after that moment I became really intolerant of anybody who got grossed out by something other people in the world ate for breakfast every day. Just shut the fuck up and eat a duck baby.

Oh, I also got fat because it was too hot to exercise. I'd wake up with my upper lip dripping with sweat. At the time, there were no gyms in Vietnam. Old people did small movements in the park to corny-ass music but that's not real exercise. That's called not being dead. No one had kettlebells and it was rare to see a female run. Young women didn't exercise to lose weight because they didn't need to. They were all so skinny, to the point where you had to wonder how their guts fit into their bodies.

One day, I tried playing volleyball with this group of male Cambodian exchange students. But according to my friend who grew up speaking Cambodian, they spent the whole time calling me mean, childish names like "big head" and "fat glasses girl" (in their defense, they hadn't seen my gigantic bush, so they had to work with what they had), so I left and never tried playing with them again. I also tried badminton but constantly lost patience with the timing of that slow-ass birdie. I tried running around Hoàn Kiếm Lake at six A.M., which was the only appropriate time to exercise since it wasn't quite as hot. But running in the dark in a foreign country was scarier than being fat. I know they say "beauty is pain" but I don't think they mean "beauty is getting robbed for your organs." Plus, even in the dark, people could recognize that I was an American. So by my second lap, I'd be surrounded by five buff men, all desperate to practice their English. They'd tell me flattering things like "You have energy like a boy" or "You don't look like you have American money." (They didn't understand that my vintage Lisa Lisa & Cult Jam T-shirt was very cool in the United States.) So instead of focusing on how to get my workout in for the day, I prioritized exploring and learning as much as I could. It made me see how much mental energy and time we spend on losing weight in the United States.

All the Việt Kiều (Vietnamese American) girls on the program, including myself, got called fat all the time. In Vietnam, strangers sitting on stools feel entitled to roast you as you walk by. One day, a girl named Phuong finally got fed up with it and responded to this guy clowning her with this horrible comeback: "Well, at least I'm not *poor*." The American, privileged, guilty part of me was mortified, but the Pussy Grabs Back part of me (which is much stronger) was like, *Go in on this dude!*

There was constant tension between a lot of Việt Kiều girls and Vietnamese people. They all thought I was a robust Japanese tourist because I dressed in baseball jerseys and wore my hair in two buns. That meant that I didn't experience a lot of the envy Vietnamese had for the Vietnamese American girls who they thought were so lucky to be born and raised in the United States. Sometimes I think they called us fat to remind us that we were no better than them just for having more money and speaking English. Also, it was a glandular thing, so shut the hell up, Quan.

––––––

My roommate, Asiroh Cham, was the only person on the program who lost weight. Her last name was Cham because, well, she was Cham. The Cham are the indigenous people of Vietnam, and her father, very smartly, instructed all the Cham people before fleeing Vietnam to change their last name to Cham so they could easily find one another in the United States. She told me that her father hated Vietnamese people and referred to them as "robbers." And when I visited her extended family's village outside of Hanoi, I could understand why he'd felt that way. His family was constantly being harassed by the police and asked for bribes.

Asiroh and I chose to do a homestay to help improve our Vietnamese, while everyone else lived in the dorms. With the exception of the one white guy on our program, all the other students grew up speaking Vietnamese. Many assume that because my dad was Chinese and my mom is Vietnamese that I am fluent in both. But instead, their ability to speak different languages canceled each other out so they only spoke English at home, because that's the only way they could communicate. It made me resent my parents a little for not making more of an effort to pass on their languages to me and my siblings. But once you two were born, I realized that it would've taken so much work for them, in addition to raising four kids. Both your dad and I speak semi-fluent Spanish and put more focus and energy into not saying "fuck" instead of teaching you "agua."

The family we stayed with had a nephew named Canh who was basically their servant. My mom says that this is really common, that every Vietnamese family living in a major city in Vietnam takes in a niece or nephew from the countryside to be their cook, house cleaner, and nanny, in exchange for food, lodging, and an education. Canh slept in a doorless room next to the entryway of the house, right next to five dogs. He cooked every single meal and put what he called

"Ajinomoto" (that's MSG) in everything. I'd stand next to him, waving flies away from the raw food, as he'd sauté tomatoes with fish sauce and garlic. Eventually, he'd always add meat or vegetables and my glasses would fog up from the savory steam. To this day, I still use tomatoes, fish sauce, and garlic as the base for most of my dishes.

Asiroh told the family she didn't eat pork or beef, which Vietnamese people have a very hard time comprehending. Either you're a "vegetarian," which is a Buddhist monk who has no sex and shaves their head and lives in the temple and eats tofu with soy sauce and water spinach for the rest of their lives, or you're a person who has sex or will eventually have sex and eats meat. Those are the only two choices of things to be. One day I was cooking with Canh (that sounds like a good TV show) and discovered that the family kept a large stock of boiled pork bones. They'd use pork fat as their cooking oil for everything, including vegetables, tofu, and soup. It certainly made everything tasty—you don't have to be Vietnamese to understand that pork fat makes everything better (like Cardi B!). I am still addicted to bacon chocolate and bacon donuts and just plain bacon. But the family had interpreted Asiroh's odd dietary restriction to mean she just didn't eat "pieces" of meat. Cooking her vegetables in meat juice seemed fine to them. And as a result, Asiroh had constant diarrhea.

As I kept moving the notches up on my belt, I grew to envy Asiroh's chronic diarrhea. We joked that she was constantly sitting atop a "Not-So-Crystal-Geyser." But then we both got diarrhea after eating at a famous Hue restaurant called "Âm Phủ," which means "Hell" in Vietnamese. Everyone studying in a developing country should, at some point, get explosive diarrhea. It's incredibly humbling and such a bonding experience. I barely knew Asiroh before the program. By the end, we were like sisters with a profound connection forged in a cauldron of diarrhea foam. Sort of like the mother-daughter bond I have with you two. Any relationship built from the foundation of diarrhea will stand the test of time.

Even though the house we stayed in was very nice, in Vietnam, you cannot escape cockroaches, mosquitoes, and epic, frothy diarrhea. Now I see Asiroh at least twice a month. We show each other our C-section scars, raise our babies together, and always joke about how some people are blood brothers, but we are shit sisters.

———

The best way to learn a new language is if you start fucking someone from that country. That's why Daddy speaks Spanish so well. He didn't learn it from la escuela, he learned it from la panocha. He had many Mexican lovers when he "studied" abroad. None of the women on my program slept with a local. I've only heard of that shit happening for women who study in Europe or Africa. Asian-from-Asia men are generally not attracted to Asian American women. They all find us too fat and loud, and they think we dress like Bratz dolls.

I was hoping to find love with someone on my program. But again, it consisted of 98 percent women. I think this is common for study-abroad programs. Women tend to be more adventurous and you have to have your shit together to go abroad. There's a lot of paperwork and fear of the unknown involved. One of the boys was another doughy white man (no thanks). And the other was a guy named Hai. From the moment I saw him, I was into it. He looked like the male version of me, which really turned me on. He wore tortoise-shell glasses, short-sleeved checkered shirts, cargo shorts, and colorful New Balance sneakers. I wanted to fuck a version of me that had a dick—the ultimate form of self-affirmation.

Hai spoke much better Vietnamese than I did, which also made him somewhat of an authority figure. No other woman on the program wanted him, because he was disgusting. He was so Jungle Asian that he rocked the infamous long pinky fingernail. I fear that the long pinky nail is going extinct. Many non-Jungle Asians wrongly assume that it's grown to support a coke habit. Hai joked that instead of a finger, he had a free, reusable Q-tip.

Every day on the van ride to school, he and I would sit in the front together, next to the driver. One morning he was picking his ear and nose like a toddler. I screamed to everyone in the back, "Hai is picking his nose!" And all of the girls in the program yelled, "Ew!" "Stop it!" "Grow up, dude!" So naturally, he turned around and flicked whatever crust came out at whoever tried to dim his light. It was like the Garbage Pail Kid's version of an Oprah giveaway. "You get a booger! You get a booger! And you get a booger!" He and I laughed so much about it that by the time I got to school my stomach was sore; I had never met anyone like him. I thought he was outrageous and *hot*.

On top of all that, he was a former bad boy. My boyfriend prior to him listened to NPR and was obsessed with *Freaks and Geeks.* Hai was from the hood in San Diego and had a tattoo of his last name, Truong, in cursive, on his arm. He had been to jail for grand theft auto in his teens, and told me about how when he first went in there, he got into a fight right away and didn't back down. He told me how important it was to stand your ground in those scenarios, because if he hadn't, the beatings would've only increased. But eventually he got his shit together and he transferred to UC Berkeley junior year. He was like a modern-day Vietnamese version of John Travolta's character in *Grease* and I wanted him to dance his way right into my bee-gee spot.

At the beginning of the semester, the program director asked if any of us were interested in volunteering at a children's hospital. Everyone raised their hands enthusiastically except for me and Hai. That was the exact moment I officially fell in love with him. He said to me: "We did not come to Vietnam to help children. We came to *help ourselves*." Which was 100 percent true. Nothing against sick children, but unless they came charging out of my vagina, I don't want to be wiping their noses and their butts. Hai was brutally honest and unapologetic. *HOT*.

I loved his sense of adventure. On the second day of the program, Hai, Asiroh, and I bought bicycles and used them as our main method of transportation instead of taxis. One night while biking around Hoàn Kiếm Lake, he and I got stuck in monsoon rain and had to pedal through brown water that came up to our knees (and reminded me of my bond with Asiroh!). Since both of us wore glasses we could barely see and fell over multiple times into the street river. Instead of complaining about getting dirty, or our shirts uncomfortably clinging to our bodies, we laughed the entire time. When he dropped me off at my homestay doorstep, I was hoping he'd finally kiss me in the rain like in the movies. Instead he just said, "That was fun, Ali," and then pedaled away.

We were spending so much time together and I had such strong feelings for him, but I couldn't tell if he was into it or not. One night, the program director took all of us out to eat snake in a village right outside of Hanoi. Now any good ethnic studies major can tell you a million different ways that *The*

Temple of Doom is problematic, from the bastardization of Hindu culture to Short Round's accent. But this was some straight Indiana Jones shit. At this restaurant, which was essentially someone's house, there were cages full of cobras. I picked one and then a man unceremoniously whipped it against the floor. Then he severed the head, which continued to move on the ground for a couple of minutes. Then he drained its blood, which was then combined with gin to drink during the meal. The snake man then slit the reptile's entire belly and grabbed the still-beating cobra heart. He dropped it in a shot glass full of gin and I wanted that heart inside me immediately. It's apparently very unusual for women to drink it. Vietnamese men generally fight over it because it's said to boost male virility, but I didn't care—I was drinking that heart. Then the snake man took out the liver and drained the black bile, which he also combined with gin to drink during the meal. He then skinned and butchered the rest of the snake right in front of us and prepared nine dishes with that one snake: fried snake, snake rinds, snake soup, steamed snake, barbecued snake, snake and corn, etc. The two girls on our program who happened to speak the best Vietnamese were horrified and refused to eat it. Instead they picked at some kernels of steamed white rice, while I rolled my eyes because the doughy white guy ate the shit out of it. Those of us who were deciding to enjoy life found out that snake is delicious. It tasted like a cross between fish, chicken, and being a fucking badass.

That snake certainly boosted my virility. That night, full of gin, bile, and snake blood, I stood outside knocking on and yelling through Hai's door, begging him to have sex with me and professing that I was madly in love with him. I was knocking so hard I almost broke the glass. Poor Asiroh had to hold me back and was probably tempted to splash water on my face to sober me up. Luckily Hai wasn't even in his room.

All of the wondering if he felt the same way was killing me. Instead of just asking him like a decent person, I decided to sneak into his dorm room and read his diary. I knew that it was a gross violation of his privacy, but love makes you crazy, and when I found an entry dedicated to me, the guilt vanished.

The entry started off great. He wrote about how much he loved spending time with me, how much fun I was, how I made him laugh. But then it quickly transitioned to this sentence: "I just don't see Ali as a sexual partner. All of that hair. On her legs, in her armpits, and on her upper lip." Thank goodness he hadn't seen my colossal bush—otherwise I'm certain that would have made the list of "problem areas."

Most people would feel motivated to do a big makeover to get the guy to like them. After all, he literally spelled out *exactly* what I needed to change. And I would have, but I was too lazy to do anything about my body hair. I didn't shave my armpits. I didn't wax my mustache, and I didn't do jack shit about my leg hair. I had also just come off that very empowering Ani DiFranco/Liz Phair summer in Hawai'i where we didn't need any man's approval and had a great fucking time. It made me angry that he couldn't just mentally slash and burn through all the hair to see that I was a very beautiful woman underneath it all. *YOU shave my body, Hai . . . with your MIND.*

A few days later, we went to a fortune-teller who was real as *fuck.* She wasn't one of those hoodwinkers who just validates wishful thinking. She told one girl on the program that her future would consist of a miscarriage, a couple abortions, and three divorces. And she got *paid* to tell her that. The poor girl was so depressed afterward she started smoking. That same fortune-teller told me I would marry a man who was the same race as me, who wore glasses, and that we would have four kids.

So I thought, *She means I'm gonna marry Hai! YAY!* All I had to do was wait for him to come to his senses. Then one day, we were lying side by side in bed, facing the ceiling, and he said, "I think we should talk about our feelings for each other." *This was it.* I was so excited that I started to panic a little. I hadn't splashed water on my vagina to wash out the pussy flakes, but this guy picked his nose in front of everyone, so whatever.

"Yes, we absolutely should," I said as I turned to him. But he stayed facing the ceiling.

"I know you have feelings for me, but I see you as more of a friend."

It broke my heart. I said, "This is torture. I can't handle this anymore." And I got up and left the room.

The next morning, I thought about not sitting next to him in the front seats of the van, but quickly realized I would only be punishing myself more if I deprived myself of that fun ride to school. Plus everyone else in the van would know something was wrong and I didn't want to draw more attention to my humiliation. It was awkward between us for the first couple of days after he banished me to The Friend Zone. But I made a decision to have fun and do my best to make amends with the classic sad reality of: He's just not that into you.

Then, a couple weeks later, right before Thanksgiving, he told me that he actually did like me. He kissed me in that same twin bed where he had rejected me earlier. For the rest of the semester, we spent a bunch of our nights in that twin bed, watching bootleg DVDs of American classics that cost one dollar on his Dell laptop. Our favorite was *Cape Fear*. We would repeat "Counselor" to each other and laugh our heads off. On the weekends we loved to explore and go shopping. We got matching backpacks, bootleg North Face jackets, and fake Nike sneakers (when we played tennis the soles flew right off). I sat in his lap as we wheeled around the country in a cyclo, being fully present in the feeling of how magical it was to fall in love in Vietnam.

When the program ended a few months later, Hai and I decided to try to continue our relationship in the States. I was in L.A., he was in Berkeley, and I always wanted to make plans to see each other. He got tired of making plans. He constantly lost important things like his passport, wallet, and keys, and I got tired of tracking them down. Soon after, we broke up.

Hai turned out to be a very nomadic man who didn't want to settle down, but we are still in each other's lives. You can be friends with ex-partners, don't believe the bullshit that you can't. If a person was once inside of you, that automatically makes them a special and unique person in your life. I mean, how many people will you ever let *inside* of you? (That's a rhetorical question. I do NOT want to know. My number is a mystery but I think it's somewhere in the teens. Yikes. Why the hell am I telling you all of this?!)

Hai lives somewhere between the Bay Area, Denver, San Diego, and Saigon. Whenever I go to Vietnam I make sure to visit him if he's living there. He'll always pick me up and drop me off at my hotel. I'll ride on the back of his motorbike and we'll reminisce about how much fun we had on that program together. We have coached and soothed one another through heartbreak over others. He's seen me through several boyfriends and supported me through my miscarriage and my father's death. He's a good friend to me.

When he's in San Diego I always make sure to see him there as well. We'll eat at a hole-in-the-wall Vietnamese restaurant on El Cajon Boulevard, where everything is under eight dollars, someone is always taking a nap on a cot behind the cash register, and everyone is in flip-flops. The last time I went, I brought my mom and Mari with me. When my mom asked Hai what he was up to, he told her that he was growing marijuana and contemplating converting a sprinter van into a home for himself. My mom smiled throughout the meal and ate her pho, nodding her head. After we said goodbye, my mom said, "Thank God you didn't marry him, Ali." I'm glad too, because otherwise we wouldn't be the great friends we are today. We would be divorced because his pinky nail gave our kids staph infections.

———

I decided to go to Vietnam because I grew up so disproportionately Chinese American. My dad was kind of an imperialist in that way, where he just dominated the culture of our home. He thought the Chinese people's contributions, culture, and history were superior and that everything Vietnamese was essentially derivative of his proud Chinese culture. To prove his point, he once said, "Name three signature characteristics of Vietnamese culture that aren't actually Chinese."

I replied, "Fish sauce, the áo dài [a traditional Vietnamese dress], and . . ."

After struggling to name a third characteristic, my dad smiled, leaned back into his brown leather chair, and said, "Exactly."

We were very distant from my mother's family because my

dad loathed my mom's siblings. She had thirteen so he was bound not to get along with a healthy percentage of them. It's a good thing that my grandma never lived to see me complain about having two kids when she had fourteen. My mom sometimes forgets which of her siblings are still alive. I don't know any Vietnamese person who doesn't have an uncle with a gambling problem and an auntie that's straight up greedy and evil. I had grown up spending the holidays with my dad's side of the family and attended this Chinatown youth center that my dad had gone to as a boy.

In our house, we ate mostly Cantonese food. We'd always eat at the same restaurant, Ming River, on Geary Boulevard, and order the same dishes every time: fillet of rock cod with bitter melon, salt baked chicken, and garlic fried ong choy. We almost never went to Vietnamese restaurants, and when we did, my mom hated how my dad would have to order through her and she'd be forced to play translator for everyone. It exhausted her. And, because most Vietnamese people in the United States are from the south of Vietnam, they often found it difficult to understand my mom's central accent. One Vietnamese man told me that listening to a Hue accent was the equivalent of someone saying "Shubba Shubba Shubba" in English when what they meant to say was "How much for extra tendon?" So it was just easier for us to go eat Chinese food.

The end result was that I was extremely familiar with where my dad grew up but had little sense of my mom's childhood home, her neighborhood, what her culture was like, how she dressed, or what she ate. She was like Don Draper except I didn't want to climb on top of her every time I saw her on-screen.

My mom visited me during my semester abroad. Getting

to see her speak with comfort and ease in her native tongue, in the country where she was born, made me really happy. But it also made me sad—I had not previously known what a confident and funny person she actually was. But it was undeniable on her home turf. She suddenly became this beaming extrovert. It made me think about the hardships she faced when she came to the United States and how she must have built up a crazy thick shell to survive. She first lived in the Midwest, where people yelled "ching chong" at her wherever she went. Then she moved to San Francisco, where she encountered Chinese people who were total snobs to her. They were my dad's friends who were born in the United States, and some of them treated my mom like mogwai from *Gremlins.* "Whatever you do, don't get water on her!"

She and I recently watched the movie *Brooklyn* together. Saoirse Ronan plays an Irish immigrant adjusting to life in the United States. My mom hated the movie and said, "That white lady going through Ellis Island was like a country club compared to my experience trying to get by in America." And when I think back on witnessing her in her home country, when she visited me, I can see what a shock and how lonely it must have been when she went to the United States—from being surrounded by all these people who look like you, talk like you, accept your existence inherently, to living permanently in a place where all the opposites are true.

When she first got here, a dentist took one look at her teeth and said she had "the mouth of a caveman." I used to think it was funny, like you might when you read that, but the truth is that American society, while being so rife with opportunity and so incredible in so many ways, also generally made her feel primitive. And I thought about all the private school parents at my school, and how it must have been so strange for her to have to socialize with them, talking about debutante balls and being pressured to donate money to a school for which she was already breaking her back to pay the tuition. Now that I am a parent at a private school, and even having grown up in that system, I find it hard to talk to those parents. And I find it excruciating to donate money to anything besides my sneaker collection fund. Imagine what *she* must have felt.

Witnessing all of those hardworking female street vendors in Vietnam also made me understand why my mom felt so passionate about me and my sisters working. While we were in Vietnam together, she explained that the country had a history of always being in wartime, so women were expected to rise to the occasion of making money for the family. Vietnamese women were always ready to take over roles traditionally filled by men, like *A League of Their Own* (but where everyone is Marla Hooch). I also understood why my mom wasn't into processing her feelings, and how she was taught to just get over tragedy. To survive, she had to believe things like depression and allergies were a choice. In a culture entrenched in wartime, those who chose to be unhappy or to refuse gluten didn't last long.

———

My mom is from Hue, a central part of Vietnam, and I got to meet a lot of her cousins who still live there. Growing up in such a small town, my mom came from this culture of extreme gossip. Everyone thrives off talking about relatives and neighbors: "Tuyet is so rich now that each of her four daughters has a Sony Discman!" "Long is marrying a smart but not so beautiful woman. Kind of like a Vietnamese Andrea Zuckerman." "The man across the street has such bad knees, he forced his poor wife to sew tiny pillows so he can kneel on them when he watches *Face/Off*." Vietnamese people demand to know how much you paid for anything because their single worst nightmare is overpaying. So part of the gossiping was them trying to productively collect pricing information because, especially back then, nothing had a set price. It was up to the people to locate the median price they should pay for an item through intensive surveying. It used to drive me crazy, how nosy my mom was. But I came to see that for her, it was a necessary way of life. Paying two dollars extra for a colander was *not* an option.

After my program ended I stayed with my mom's cousin, who lived with her mother, sisters, daughters, and husband in Hue. It was powerful to experience many generations living under one roof. I am not used to living with someone who is ninety but everyone in Vietnam, at some point, lives with a grandma who is ninety years old. There is no such thing as an "old folks home" in Vietnam. The senior citizens' rec center is just their house, where they raised their kids and help raise their grandkids. When you become an adult, you learn to become a caretaker of your parents, the way they took care of you when you were a child. There is a huge benefit to having all of those generations living in one house. There's so much oral history passed down from grandparents, but maybe more important, there's built-in childcare. Grandparents in Vietnam take care of their grandkids and it keeps them active and stimulated. They also take care of their daughters and daughters-in-law when they have babies (for free!). Being a new mother isn't such a lonely experience because you have your own mother and/or your mother-in-law right there in your own home. I thought about this so much when I first had Mari. I tried to replicate it as best I could by surrounding myself with

as many women as possible and planning for my family to visit
often for support. But it's also probably super annoying to
have your mom in your house permanently, let's be real. I
mean nothing is free. I max out when Grandma stays more
than four nights. I know she seems nice, but she insists on
microwaving a bowl of leftovers covered in plastic wrap when
I have told her a thousand times that plastic is gonna melt and
kill us!

After the time I spent in Hue with my mom's cousin and
her house with eighteen generations still alive in it somehow,
I went to live with Auntie Nga in Saigon. She was my mom's
only sibling that had returned to Vietnam after studying in
the United States. She lived in a tiny one-bedroom house and
spoke perfect English. She would gossip about how one of
her and my mom's uncles would mess around with different
women in his younger years and had a bunch of sexually
transmitted diseases from it. She'd refer to him as "mango
seeds," which is a very poetic interpretation of what "raging
genital warts" look like. Auntie Nga had two daughters my
age, and I wished so badly that we had grown up together in
the United States. They were so kind and loved to sing karaoke. Our favorite song was "La Bamba" because we thought
it was so funny how we could just repeat "Para bailar La
Bamba" over and over again. My cousin Titi spent a ton of
time in the bathroom because it was the only place she could
be alone and have some privacy. But my aunt would knock on
the door to rush Titi out and say, "Hurry up, Mrs. Masturba-
tor."

Auntie Nga would only speak to me in English because
she desperately wanted her daughters to learn the language.
And while I was having a great time, it made me feel really
fortunate to have been born and raised in the United States,

with an American education. Auntie Nga had to work so hard to teach her children to think critically. At the time in Vietnam, education was all about rote memorization. Especially now, with the Internet and Wikipedia, it's a totally useless skill. It's not an advantage at all, to have all of that information memorized. I was raised to ask why, to learn how to process information and think for myself. Knowing the capital of Mozambique and being able to fill in the entire periodic table of the elements does not give you an advantage these days when there's Google. It's more important to know how to pick a news program (hint: It's not the one that has to dole out millions of dollars in sexual harassment lawsuits) and good friends (hint: It's not that asshole boy at the park who throws sand and keeps licking the monkey bars).

———

Before your father, I had dated a couple of guys that were very scared of getting out of their comfort zone and could have greatly benefited from studying abroad. My senior year of college, I took a class on documentary filmmaking. I had a huge crush on my T.A. Superficially, he was the whole package: smart, articulate, funny, passionate, Asian American, nose piercing, and fucking *ripped*. Before class I would do leg lifts to tighten my core, and if I saw him walking around on campus, I'd scurry off to the nearest bathroom to check that I didn't look gross. If I did, in fact, look gross, I'd walk in the opposite direction from him. But I never thought he'd be interested in someone like me. I biked around campus in huge cargo pants, wearing a backward SF Giants hat and a T-shirt that read SUCKA FREE.

But I did such a great job on my final project that my T.A. slept with me (which is like extra extra extra credit). I fell in love very hard and fast, but I had gotten a scholarship to an intensive language program in Vietnam and was leaving to go back there after graduation. We handwrote each other letters that were sometimes twelve pages long. His letters made me laugh. Once he drew a before/after stick figure of me with a mammoth curly bush and then after, having by then trimmed it back considerably (upon his request). He'd tell me how much he'd think about me when listening to Tracy Chapman's "The Promise." (The best song when you're longing for somebody, and possibly the greatest song ever made? Anyway, listen to Tracy Chapman. That bitch knows what it's like to miss somebody and make them promise to wait for your ass!) And eventually, he came to Vietnam to visit me. I was so excited, but the man had never been to Southeast Asia. He had never backpacked. He was scared to ride motorbikes and eat food from street vendors (those two things are 99 percent of what Southeast Asia is all about). Tired of playing tour guide two weeks into his trip, I threw the Lonely Planet in his face and said, "It's your turn to plan today." Many times, I thought about ditching him in Cambodia. At Angkor Wat, I was very tempted to say "Hey! Look over there, it's ANOTHER phallic statue!" and then quickly catch the next flight to Hong Kong. Unlike Hai, he was less concerned with enjoying the adventure and more obsessed with his body and maintaining his BMI. In our tiny hostel room, he led me in a home workout routine he developed. He slammed a deck of cards on the concrete floor, and instructed me to turn over the first card. It was a ten of diamonds, which meant that we both then had to do ten push-ups. He flipped over the next card, which was a jack of spades. So then we both had to do eleven sit-ups. In between panting breaths of the second and third push-up, I said, "Man, I'm pretty out of shape. This is hard! I think I've gained too much weight to do this." He was supposed to say, "No way! You look bangin', babe! Like Rosie Perez in *Do the Right Thing*!" But instead, he replied: "It's because of all that fruit you're eating." Like, dude, shut the fuck up. Criticizing someone for eating too much fruit means you've crossed the line from health nut to health Nazi. Adam and Eve ate fruit all the time and look at what absolute legends they turned out to be. My point is, girls, that if you don't go abroad, you'll become a provincial gym rat like that guy.

Studying in a developing/third-world country is way more intense and formative than studying in a first-world fancy country. It makes you so much more open-minded, adaptive, and confident. You become so much more real. When you have to shit on two little bricks into a hole the size of a tennis ball at an elementary school in the countryside, or sleep in a farmer's yurt after not bathing for five days, you become a much more easygoing person. It teaches you to value experience over material things real fast.

And living in a different part of the world can sometimes present the opportunity to take on a new personality. I don't think I could've let myself grow out my armpit hair and gain all that weight while living in Los Angeles. People on campus would've stared at me, and I would've felt so much peer pressure to pay more attention to my appearance. If I had tried to talk to that T.A. while rocking some long, flowing pit hair, he would've probably lured me into a cage with some peanut butter and dropped me off at the no-kill shelter.

It was really moving to experience being a foreigner in the country that your mother grew up in. And it's empowering to be in a place where everyone looks like you. But I realized I kind of had that already at UCLA and in San Francisco. In

San Francisco everyone looked even *more* like me and, ultimately, I missed my tribe. I had stayed with Auntie Nga in Vietnam for a couple of months after the semester abroad ended and learned very quickly that I wouldn't want to live there forever. I got worn down by the constant negotiation. The bargaining. Sometimes a bundle of cilantro costs an entire dollar and that's okay! All the blatant opinions. How everything is a struggle. The heat. I began to appreciate the diversity in America. I missed listening to hip-hop on the radio while driving. I missed tacos. And there was a dismissal of women in Asia; actually, the men were the main reason I wanted to go home. They talked down to me. They laughed me off when I tried to play sports with them or drink at the table with them. I got sick of mosquito bites and the monsoons that would make my money wet and my shoes squishy.

And I also really missed the American sense of humor. It was hard for Vietnamese people to understand my jokes because the concept of sarcasm doesn't exist in Vietnam. The height of funny for them was when a man dressed up like a woman and nagged her husband. Basically those Madea movies, but with less rolling pins.

If you girls end up studying in Vietnam (please), and I come visit you on your program (I will), you best believe that I'll be out until two A.M., reminiscing with Hai about that time I ate a still-beating cobra heart.

CHAPTER 7

The DJ

Dear Girls,

This is going to be a short letter but it's important because I don't want you to repeat my mistake.

I have always been attracted to men who dress hip-hop. I grew up in the nineties worshipping Aaliyah, Missy Elliott, Wu-Tang Clan, Lauryn Hill, Tupac, and A Tribe Called Quest. There's no better music to dance to than hip-hop, and no better music to listen to when you're going through anything emotional than R&B. (No genre of music videos features more sensual candles than R&B. It's very comforting.) I found it very hard to connect with anyone who didn't agree with my music tastes. I have never liked men who wear bowling shirts on the off chance it might mean they would want to blast Smash Mouth while eating dino chicken nuggets for breakfast. I have also never ever been attracted to men that wear eyeliner because then I would be subjected to marathons of David Lynch movies and forced to listen to Pink Floyd's *Dark Side of the Moon* played backward. In the nineties there was this awful category of raver men that wore goggles and wide-legged fluorescent yellow pants and would dance like Teletubbies on acid. I would give any man in need of style help a hip-hop makeover. The clothes are very flattering because they inject instant masculinity and can give volume to a skinny dude's body.

My favorite hip-hop guy has always been the DJ, never the rapper. That might be partially due to the fact that I'm into Asian men and grew up near Daly City, where every hot Filipino practices one of the ancient art forms of Pinoy culture: DJing, breakdancing, or nursing. Rappers are generally megalomaniacs because their job is to rap about how great they are. It always felt strange to see grown men rhyme like that. In high school they would gather in these freestyle circles and "cipher" with their very prepared, very written, non-improvised raps. A common rhyme I heard was "the colonization of this nation" . . . coming from the white child of a venture capitalist attending a $30K per year high school. Recently, a friend who raps wanted to share with me one of his latest verses. Before I could have any time to say "no thanks," he just started rapping and gesturing furiously in front of my face. I did my best to tune out but he kept looking me in the eye. One of his most memorable lines: "I write psalms, not rap songs." It's memorable because he paused after this line. I thought he was finished but then he faced his palms up to the sky and raised his eyebrows. Really, he was just waiting for my reaction to his genius play on the word "psalms" unexpectedly rhyming with "songs." And it was kind of like a psalm because after that I was like, *Jesus save me.* But I felt bad and just said, "Dayuuuuuuuuuum," which fortunately made him feel good but unfortunately encouraged him to continue rapping for five more minutes. It was so awkward and I felt like I was being held hostage. Out of fear of being rude, it took a hundred percent of my willpower to resist the instinct to look away and scream, "You're not Eminem in *8 Mile*! I'm not Brittany Murphy and you don't work in a steel factory! Xzibit is nowhere to be found! Stop rapping!" There's nothing like having your time be assaulted by a grown man's rhymes. That's why I have always preferred DJs. You get the hip-hop performer without the obnoxious poet. They know how and when to shut up. Plus they can play weddings, which pay actual money, so you don't have to support their rhyming asses.

DJs also have the opportunity to really showcase how good they are with their hands. When they place that needle, scratch that record, adjust the fader, I just can't help myself. All of that *finger work*. And then they always move their hips to the subtle beat of the song that not everybody else is dancing to. It's like they have some extraterrestrial ability to hear a secret dog whistle hidden inside the music. It's sexy when a man is passionate about something because you think that passion will translate into the bedroom. You've already witnessed him being committed to *something*. His passion also becomes healthy competition. The goal is to become so irresistible to him that you're the one thing that can pull him away from crate digging and record scratching.

In my early twenties, I had a huge crush on this underground DJ from Los Angeles, who I'll just refer to as "that fucking DJ." I already had a fetish for turntable men, and then on top of that he looked like a Filipino James Franco (lots of cute wincing). He was like an exotic hip-hop bird that could pull off wearing a beanie just on the tip of his head, like a yarmulke. Whenever we crossed paths, he laughed *a lot*.

And when we took pictures together, he'd hug me from be-hind with his arms around my neck, which made my boy-friend at the time extremely angry. My boyfriend knew that I had a crush and forbade me from seeing him. He got very upset whenever he caught me scrolling through the DJ's Myspace page. One night the DJ texted me that he was in San Francisco performing, and I very badly wanted to go but I knew my boyfriend wouldn't let me. So I snuck out like a teenager in a family sitcom. I wore a denim miniskirt and a tight red tank top under sweatpants and a sweatshirt and pre-tended I was going to my parents' house to do laundry. In my car, I changed out of my sweatpants, put on knee-high leather boots and makeup, and let down my hair. I did not cheat. I just saw the DJ, went to the back to hang out, and then drove home. Sure, it was extremely deceitful and went against my boyfriend's exact wishes, but no body fluids were exchanged and nobody was penetrated so I felt all good in the morality hood.

When my boyfriend and I finally broke up months later, I changed my Myspace relationship status from "In a Relation-ship" to "Single." In the early 2000s, that was our way of put-ting the bat signal out for dick. It would show up in people's newsfeeds and I was hoping the DJ would take notice. It was the sexual Amber Alert of our times. He called me immedi-ately, telling me that he was in town, and asked if he could come spend the night at my apartment. Cue: *Oh yeeeeeah* sound effect from *Ferris Bueller's Day Off*.

I quickly changed into a lacy camisole and pajama pants and made sure to wear makeup that didn't look too overtly like I was so excited to finally fuck this DJ who had been off the table for way too long. I rushed over to the toilet to trim my pubes, stuck one foot up on the sink, and splashed my vagina with some water (which became inspiration for some of my finest stand-up work). His friends dropped him off and we talked on my couch in the living room for a while. Again, he was laughing laughing laughing at everything I said, and at first I thought, *Okay, um, yeah, he's just getting to know me a little more and is trying to be a gentleman.* But by the second hour of talking I started to grow tired and impatient. By the third hour I was like, *What the fuck is this dude waiting for?* and asked him if he wanted to go to my bedroom, and leaned in for a kiss.

He leaned back and replied that he just wanted to be friends. Cue: extremely loud record scratch.

Prior to this, I had been broken up with. I had flirted with a man only to not have that flirtation reciprocated. I even had that whole Hai thing where I was madly in love with him but then read his journal entry about how long my armpit hair was and how he found me as sexually desirable as Eric Stoltz in that movie with Cher where he played a red-headed boy with a funky face. But never, ever had I made a physical move on a man and been flat-out rejected.

At the time, I felt like he led me on. I was like a male harassment monster from a #MeToo story: *What did he expect, coming over to my apartment for God's sake?! Did he actually think that I said yes to him coming over just to hang out? I am entitled to a hookup godddahhhmmmmeeet.* The difference is that I did not show my anger explicitly. No man is ever coerced into hooking up with a woman because he's scared she's going to be mad if he just wants to hang out. And I didn't persist after he told me no because that would've been pathetic. I could never imagine harassing a man until he finally gave in. How could I even get off, knowing that getting his pants off took *convincing*? If a man rejects you once you've physically made a move on him, he's not going to change his mind. The dick don't lie. I don't want him to kiss me because I wore him down. That orgasm is not worth the price I would have paid with my ego. I played off his rejection like it didn't affect me because I was trying to preserve some dignity in this nightmare of an evening.

Then he told me that he was a virgin for religious reasons, and when he said that, I was so grateful we didn't have sex. Like, no thank you. I don't want to have the remains of your innocence in my vagina! He would've ejaculated with extreme guilt and potentially cried right after. A wasted number on my already too long list.

So please don't ever have sex with a virgin man unless you yourself are a virgin. And if you do have sex with another virgin, prepare to be wildly disappointed. They take seven minutes to put on a condom and then take forty seconds to cum. There is zero allure in taking a grown man's virginity. They might not have a physical hymen that you can break and make them bleed, but their emotional hymen is real, and it's thick, especially at that age. In fact, taking a grown man's virginity is such a burden that, after that, I never pursued another DJ again for fear he might also be a virgin. Unless you're a vampire trying to eat fresh, or a witch with a shopping list, virgins are just too much to handle.

CHAPTER 8

Mr. Wong

Dear Girls,

Whenever possible, I try to coordinate matching outfits for me and your father. We have matching black puff vests, matching Nike sweatpants, matching Allbirds shoes, and matching Hokusai print T-shirts from Uniqlo. I used to not understand why older Asian couples dressed alike. Some people think it's because they're slowly becoming the same person—an elderly, wise, balding, cheap, tai-chi-loving, ginseng-obsessed tortoise. But I have Daddy wear the same clothes as me in order to claim him. A wedding ring is not enough and him wearing a T-shirt that says TEAM ALI is a little bit tacky. I don't want any bitch to be misled into thinking that he's snatchable. Some might think it's a bit possessive, I prefer to view it as a reflection of my love, and how much I value him.

When I met your father in 2009, he was taking a year off

from business school. After a string of losers, I was so excited to date someone from Harvard. Finally, somebody who owned a printer and a garlic press! The first time he invited me back to his apartment, I couldn't wait. I assumed he lived in a spacious one-bedroom in the West Village, with some Moroccan poufs, an open-concept kitchen full of stainless steel appliances, and maybe even a Vitamix!

Well, as it turned out, Daddy lived in a closet. No, he wasn't gay. He lived in an *actual* closet in the East Village. You had to go through Daddy's roommate's room to get to Daddy's room, because Daddy's room was the closet of his roommate's room. Immediately when you walked in the closet, there was a ladder to get to Daddy's bed, which was a platform that only had space for his mattress and laptop. Underneath the platform was where he stored all of his belongings and got dressed. It was like a treehouse of ancestral disappointment. Since there was nowhere to eat in Daddy's closet, we ate breakfast on the roommate's bed after the roommate had gone to work. His roommate did healing work with very powerful magnets so we couldn't have our cellphones in that room or our text messages and personal info would go to outer space. I acted like I was totally cool with all this, but in my head, I was like, *Motherfucker, I thought you went to SIDWELL with Chelsea Clinton!*

But this adult man who grew up in a mansion with so much privilege never complained about these odd living conditions. He decorated it with Christmas lights and photos from his time in the Philippines, and made an altar by his bed. It showed me right away that he was a grounded person, someone who could make the most out of a shitty situation, and it really surprised me and made me wonder what else he had to reveal.

Every time we hung out, I thought, *Who* is *this guy?* During the day we'd go to yoga together and eat hummus for lunch. Then at night, I'd come home to him after doing a stand-up show, and he'd be sitting in that closet watching an intense, violent movie on his laptop. He was so seemingly zen but then chose to unwind with *Reservoir Dogs*. Like, dude, *what* is going on inside of you? Is there possibly an *Eyes Wide Shut* sex party demon in there I don't know about? Or a Barbra Streisand underground mall full of dolls? Because all of that would be kind of cool! All of his contradictory personality traits and interests just kept on revealing themselves to me, and kept surprising me. He kept me in a constant state of confusion and fascination that remains to this day.

For my twenty-seventh birthday, I was really looking forward to your father's gift. I told myself, *Guys who go to Harvard Business School don't fuck around. His peers know how to give great gifts to their trophy wives and I'm well on my way to becoming one, so I am totally ready for the Hermès box with the Birkin bag inside.* But there was no box. There was no bag with tissue peeking out of the top. We sat down on his bed, in his closet room, as he gave me an envelope. It must be a gift card to Cartier! Even better! He's letting *me* choose between rose gold and white gold! But there was no gift card inside. Instead, there was a blank card with these instructions: "Write down all of your goals." Then he had me recite them back to him. And after every goal I read out loud to him, he replied, "So it shall be." Like a cheap-ass genie, he gave me homework for my birthday. I shook the envelope upside down to see if there was anything else inside. At the time I would've preferred a Burberry fanny pack, something I could actually feel in my hands and show off to people. I remember writing things like "I want to go to the Montreal Just for

Laughs Comedy Festival," "I want to heal my rosacea," and "I want to make a living off of telling jokes." Looking back, each one of those goals came true. Sometimes I think he might actually be a genie and sometimes I think I might be a hardworking funny person and that shit would've happened anyway, and now his gift just seems prescient by sheer happenstance. But honestly, it was so refreshing to be with someone so dedicated to self-reflection and self-discovery. And despite having put anal beads up another grown man's ass in a previous relationship, I had never experienced any activity that was so intimate. And straight up free.

———————

In 2011, I got invited to do *The Tonight Show* to perform my very first stand-up set on late-night TV. Until that point, my only other TV appearance was when I guest starred as Christian Slater's assistant on a Fox comedy called *Breaking In*. I was so excited because many people's careers in comedy, such as Ellen DeGeneres's or Joan Rivers's, had taken off after a *Tonight Show* appearance. It was considered the best exposure that could lead to sitcom deals and instant success. But the problem was that the date they assigned me was Daddy's graduation from Harvard Business School.

I have missed many friends' weddings, baby showers, bachelorette parties. But I'm very proud that I was smart enough not to miss your father's Harvard Business School graduation. It wasn't that hard of a decision, because I knew, in the end, he was more important. We had been dating for two years and it was already so obvious that I could never find someone else like him. Besides having a very fundamental emotional connection and physical attraction, your father and I are both the *exact same amount of Asian*. And I don't mean that it was challenging to find another full-blooded Asian person (there are over a billion in China alone). Culturally, I was yearning for someone who matched both my love for authentic Asian cuisine and also grew up going to bar mitzvahs and Passover dinners. It was always a struggle to find a partner who matched my passion for saving money, taking risks, and being engaged in anything that was challenging but ultimately worthwhile. Someone who had a high threshold for failure and a zero-tolerance policy for shoes in a house.

When I met your father, I was concerned that he was a little bit too much of a private school Asian. We West Coast Asians often have this assumption that East Coast Asians are not as evolved in their ethnic identity. That as a result of growing up around predominantly white people, they tend to be a little more ashamed of their race, overly excited to assimilate, and late in finding their place in an Asian American community. I also referred to these men as Lacrosse Asians. The few East Coast Asians I had met wore polo shirts and ate brie as a snack. When they saw footage or photographs of Japanese Americans being sent to internment camps during WW2, they thought: *Ooh, I wonder where they bought those form-fitting khakis . . .*

And the truth is that he *was* a little too much of a private school Asian at first. When your father first met my parents, I told him to make sure to bring them fruit. He arrived at their house in cargo pants, a red Adidas jacket, and a backpack. When I greeted him at the gate, I was less concerned with his music-festival-attendee outfit and more curious about where the goddamn fruit was. He smiled and reassured me, "It's in my backpack!" I led him upstairs to the kitchen, where my mom and dad were sitting next to their pistachio-green refrigerator, watching *Judge Judy* on their tiny Sony kitchen TV. They stood up, excited to meet the first guy I had brought home in years. As he answered questions about where he was born and went to college, I nudged him and whispered to him through a smile, "The fruit. Bust out the fruit." And out of his backpack, he placed on the kitchen table two bananas, a plum, a red apple, and a satsuma. My parents didn't even say thank you. They were too busy staring at the conga line of odd fruit, confused. I was like, *Shit. Were East Coast Asians not raised to understand that you're supposed to bring a giant sack of oranges, an orchid, or an overwhelming box of Asian pears? Bananas! Seriously?! Those are perhaps the most insulting part, because they are the carnations of fruit. Everyone knows they cost nineteen cents each at Trader Joe's. I think they're the only thing you can get for nineteen cents these days. One red apple?! Did he steal that from the lobby of a Howard Johnson?*

Before meeting me, he had never been to a Costco, which is like church for Asian people. He never bought anything on sale because he fell for that propaganda "You Get What You Pay For," which is the most sacrilegious thing you can say to a Chinese person. And he didn't love pork since he was a vegan. But I fixed all that. After a little while, he understood the value of only buying things on sale and gave up eating all-soy everything. After the sixth time he watched me eat chicken pho while he ate noodles in broth (that was boiled broccoli stock), he was over it. I also sent him articles every day about how eating too much soy will make a man grow titties and cause dementia. Thank you, Internet, for making it easy for me to instill fear into my boyfriend for positive change. Now he has fully come home to his Filipino carnivorous roots. We fight over the dark meat of the turkey during

Thanksgiving, share tripe, and eat our pig's feet to the bone like injured wolves who'll do anything to survive. I cannot imagine being with someone you have to battle over where to eat. All we do is eat Asian food and shop at Asian grocery stores on the weekend. And I appreciate that I don't have to defend why a bean belongs in a dessert. Most Southeast Asian desserts consist of some beans, seeds, and tapioca swimming in coconut milk. You eat it with a spoon and it's not a cake or a cookie, it's magic.

———

My ex-boyfriend Chris Garcia once said about your dad: "You can never leave that guy. He's shaman to ramen." What he meant was that there's no other living man who is the same level of hippie-dippie and Asian American, a man that shares appreciation for both the empirical and the supernatural while being Asian. Your dad was doing ayahuasca way before it was cool, and took me to do a ceremony several times. Ayahuasca is a psychedelic plant mixture that helps you heal and find answers to the questions that have been burning inside of you. At the time, I had very bad rosacea on my cheeks. My face looked like a cluster of erupting volcanoes. A shaman at the first ceremony in Tulum told me, "Your body is punishing you for thinking that you're ugly." I had gained a bunch of weight in NYC and was feeling down on myself, so he was right.

During the ceremony, we took turns drinking a cup of medicine from the shaman. It tasted exactly like what it was: boiled bark and leaves. I sat crossed-legged, quiet in a circle with your dad and a bunch of mostly Mexican women, anxiously waiting to see the tie-dye come alive in my brain. But nothing happened. So I went up to the shaman for another cup of medicine. And another and another. I lay down and stared up at the straw roof of the yurt, feeling like this whole thing was a sham and that "shaman" really meant "sham man." And as the shaman continued to sing songs in Spanish and play his acoustic guitar, I closed my eyes, and suddenly, streaks of the most beautiful colors began to shoot out like a fountain to the tune of the music. A double of myself appeared. Another Ali Wong with the same jet-black hair, glasses, and tan skin took my hand and guided me toward a barn, where she laid me down on a stack of hay.

"Take off your panties," she commanded.

"When?"

"Right now," she answered as she smiled.

"Why?"

She climbed on top of me, pulled back my hair, and whispered into my ear: "Because I said so."

She proceeded to climb down, put her head between my thighs, and stuck her tongue in my pussy. As I moaned, probably out loud in front of everyone else in the yurt, some of whom were throwing up their past traumas (instead of getting head from me, like me!), the other Ali Wong crawled on top of me, still with her tongue in my pussy, but now with *her pussy* in my face. I recognized that same white heart-shaped birthmark on the inside of her left thigh, and kissed it lovingly as I made my way to her clitoris. We rolled around together and laughed, our lips moving around each other's necks, biting each other's double-pierced earlobes, touching each other, and complimenting each other's features (which yes, were all just my features).

"Your skin is so soft."

"I love how you look when your hair drapes over your breasts."

"Your hands smell like garlic."

"Yours do too."

"They always smell like garlic because I love cooking with garlic."

"Me too."

She made me laugh, and she made me feel beautiful and gave me a lot of pleasure. And throughout my hallucination, I still saw all of those beautiful spiraling and shooting streams of turquoise mixed with orange, turning into purple and red, riding the rhythm of the music. I smiled, tears streaming down my face, because I didn't even know that this was exactly what I had come all the way to Tulum for. This hallucination actually happened, by the way. I'm not making it up for this book.

Months later, my skin cleared up. Because I took antibiotics. But still! The self-love I gained after that trip was incredible. But please take antibiotics if you need to.

During that first ceremony, I found a way to get over my physical insecurities. The second time I learned to accept my dad's death. You never really get over the death of a parent. Ayahuasca ceremonies are not always fun—I cried a lot during the second one and experienced so much grief in my hallucination. I felt how much my father was suffering when he was sick, and why eventually he probably just wanted to pass. Losing him is still the hardest thing I've ever had to cope with. And if it wasn't for your father encouraging me to take the time out to deal with it, I'm sure I would still be in a terrible place emotionally.

The second hardest thing I've ever had to cope with was my miscarriage. Your father held my hand through the entire experience, and afterward, we made the most out of me not being pregnant, and went to do mushrooms in Ojai.

In writing all of this out, it's become pretty clear to me that your dad is basically my drug dealer who happens to have exquisite taste in ramen.

————

Sometimes I fantasize about what my life would be like if I had married Idris Elba. He would talk dirty to me in a British (or is it Australian?) accent in bed and almost crush me by accident with his beautiful biceps, and I would do a very good job of pretending that I cared about his DJing career. Any married woman who hasn't fantasized about leaving her husband for Idris Elba is either lying or has extremely poor taste or is an Amish lady who has never watched *The Wire*. But then I snap out of it and realize that I wouldn't have had you two if I'd ended up with Idris. I also wouldn't have the career that I have now if it wasn't for your father.

My life changed dramatically after my first Netflix special, *Baby Cobra*, premiered. A lot of those jokes were inspired by your dad and his absurd and surprising behavior. Daddy continues to be my muse. He recently took me down an Adele YouTube wormhole that lasted an hour and moved me to tears while he supplemented the clips with all of these interesting Adele facts that I never knew. "Did you know that she wished she never watched the Amy Winehouse documentary?" "She supposedly is going to stop touring because she doesn't like applause." Unfortunately, there is no word for a man that is a muse, but there should be. How about we call him a "magnum"? Hopefully, that word and its association with the big dick condoms counterbalance the emasculating potential of being viewed as a male muse.

It's very uncommon for female comedians to tour with their children. But I wanted to bring both of you plus Daddy on the road because I didn't want to spend any nights apart. None of that would have worked without him. He decided to sell posters after the show as a way of being with me while I did shows. After *Baby Cobra,* the first theater I headlined was in Boston, in the middle of winter. He set up his poster-selling station right by the door, where it was freezing cold, and he had to wear a giant Uniqlo down jacket with a hat and earmuffs. To prepare, he bought a bunch of tablets and square readers and got a ton of posters printed. He bought a pack-able dolly on Amazon and loaded it up with boxes to take to the venue. And in that first theater run, he sold enough post-ers to pay for Mari's childcare for a month.

You will never know true suffering until you fly cross-country with a baby or a toddler. First class is almost worse because there are so many entitled, cranky old rich people who think they're paying to travel through the sky in a private, soundproof champagne bubble, when they are actually sitting in a section that is *open for purchase to the general public.* One time, Mari was singing "How Far I'll Go" from *Moana* be-cause it's the fucking jam and I feel like singing it all the time too. A sixty-year-old woman who looked like she shit caviar was sitting behind me and maliciously said "Shhhh!" at Mari while kicking my chair with her wrinkled foot. I stood up, turned around, and asked, "Are you kidding me?! She's just singing. She's a little kid." With her giant green Dolce & Gab-bana bag in her lap, she pursed her shriveled lips and said, "I know, I have two. And they have children who are much more well-behaved." I don't remember much after that. I went dark and said some words like "bitch" and "your grandkids are probably well-behaved around you because they're scared of their evil old witch of a Grandma." I would have said "old cunt" but Mari was there.

Besides the inevitable altercations with fellow passengers on the plane, dealing with explosive baby poo in such a tight space is extremely challenging. The bathrooms have a changing table that folds above the toilet, so if you're not holding both of your baby's ankles in one hand like you're about to toss them into a volcano as a human sacrifice, your baby will fall into that nasty blue plane water. You have to squeeze the new diaper and wipes in between your legs or underneath your armpits because there's no surface on which to place them in that bathroom. And your dad changed all of Mari's poo diapers on the plane while I binge-watched *Veep* and did my best to save my voice for that night's shows. Anytime he complained, I again mimicked having the C-section by taking an imaginary knife in my hand and slicing it across my C-section scar. I *still* use that trick. I used it while writing this chapter when I had to concentrate and needed Daddy's help with you two. I have no idea how much mileage I can get out of it, but it's so good that, if it expires in ten years, I might have another C-section to renew my rights to be lazy. No baby, just the C-section.

It's not easy for a man to be with a female stand-up comedian. Men are not accustomed to a woman being gone every night and hanging out with mostly men—men who are *professionally* charismatic. But Daddy never makes me feel bad when I want to do a show instead of staying home to binge-watch *Narcos* and getting asked a million questions about where everything is in the house. He's very helpful, but he will never know where the lint rollers or your swimsuits are.

During the summer of 2018, I filmed the first movie that I starred in and co-wrote, *Always Be My Maybe*. It shot in Vancouver for six weeks. During the week, I was working fourteen-hour days. I didn't want to travel back to Los Angeles on the weekends because I needed those days to sleep. So Daddy flew back and forth every weekend, going through customs, to be with all of us in our two-bedroom apartment in Vancouver. For me, getting to see the two of you while shooting that movie, even for just a couple of minutes, every day, meant so much. And it wouldn't have been possible without him. He did that, and also went on tour with me after *Baby Cobra,* all while holding down a job as the VP at a multi-billion-dollar tech company based in Los Angeles. He never slept on planes and often went to bed late at night because he was constantly having to work on his laptop when he wasn't in the office. Before, one of the things I really loved about him was that he was such a quiet, peaceful sleeper. He used to sleep like his heart was pumping natural Ambien through his body. I kept expecting to be called down to the morgue to identify him, only to have him wake up halfway through and be like, "Oh hi, I must have dozed off there." But midway through the tour after *Baby Cobra,* he started snoring from extreme exhaustion, to the point where the bed would shake and I would end up under the desk of my room at the Boise Sheraton, bracing myself for an earthquake.

Daddy and I have an agreement that instead of all the household duties falling on one person, it rotates. Some days he comes first. Some days stand-up comes first. But you two girls *always* come first for both of us.

It's easy to attend a women's march or wear a #TimesUp pin or talk about how Janet Jackson shouldn't have been shamed for revealing her nipple at the Super Bowl. But a true feminist husband doesn't see a woman's money, power, and/or respect as a reflection of his own lack of success. A true feminist husband embraces his wife's ability to provide by celebrating her and stepping up. Doing 50 percent of the childcare and household duties is simply not enough when I'm on set twelve hours per day shooting a movie. Being a woman's biggest cheerleader means breaking out of the tit for tat mentality when it comes to tasks. It's not just saying "Yay YOU!" It's taking out the trash, signing up the kids for after-school activities, packing lunch for the kids, taking them to the doctor when necessary, always making sure the minivan is full of gas, waiting at home for the exterminator, paying bills. Supporting a woman can be tedious and boring but so can *being* a working mom.

A reporter once asked me why I think progressive men who earn significantly less than their breadwinning wives still won't quit their jobs to take care of their children. Why do they still hold on to their careers, even if taking care of the children would make more financial sense because the cost of childcare is higher than their net salary?

I think I know the answer to that now, and it sucks. Women are not expected to live a life for themselves. When women dedicate their lives to children, it is deemed a worthy and respectable choice. When women dedicate themselves to a passion outside of the family that doesn't involve worshipping their husbands or taking care of their kids, they're seen as selfish, cold, or unfit mothers. But when a man spends hours grueling over a craft, profession, or project, he's admired and seen as a genius. And when a man finds a woman who worships him, who dedicates her life to serving him, he's lucky. But when a man dedicates himself to taking care of his children it's seen as a last resort. That it must be because he ran out of other options. That it's plan Z. That it's an indicator of his inability to provide for his family. Basically, that he's a fucking loser. I think it's one of the most important falsehoods we need to shatter when talking about women's rights.

I feel like I've painted maybe too rosy a picture. Our marriage is straight up not perfect. Sometimes it feels like a task-driven relationship. Since I'm the messier one, at times it's like he's just listing off all the things I need to clean up or deal with. And it is true that he constantly has to put my gym bag into the basket or put my suitcase in the garage. The spaces that we don't share, like my car or trailer, are abject disasters that look like crack dens. Once a week we have this argument:

Daddy: "Please do not hang your rubber dishwashing gloves from the kitchen sink."

Me: "That's the standard place to hang them. That's where dishwashing gloves have always been hung since the beginning of dishwashing gloves. That's like saying don't put your toilet paper on the toilet paper roll."

Daddy: "But they always fall down into the sink."

Me: "Then just put them back. They're rubber gloves that weigh less than a pencil."

Daddy: "But it's one more thing for me to do."

Me: "I want a divorce."

In our weaker moments, we're constantly keeping track of marriage points. If he has a free day to hike solo while I'm at some sticky kids' birthday party with Nikki strapped to my chest, making sure Mari doesn't get accidentally smothered by ten-year-old boys in the bouncy house, then he owes me. That gives me license to sleep in until eight A.M. (that's eleven A.M. for you people without kids). We go to couple's therapy every Friday morning at nine A.M. because it's cheaper than a divorce. There's always something for us to talk about. One Mother's Day, we went out to Din Tai Fung for brunch with both of our mothers and some friends. I paid for everything and then we went to the mall, where I gave our mothers carte blanche at Sephora. At one point, I punched Daddy in the arm and said, "Hey! You wanna kick in at some point? You wanna get the moms something? Get me, who is also a mom, something?" He replied, "Well, I don't know what you want." And I screamed, "We're at a fucking *mall*. Tiffany is right there, go in and ask me if I want something and you'll find out!"

When I was little, I used to pee in my pants from laughing. They kept a pack of underwear for me at school (which I hope, if I get more famous, will become the "Ali Wong Commemorative Underwear Initiative" and future generations of pee-laughers will be safe from the embarrassment of having to throw their underwear away in a school trash can during lunch). I thought it went away until very recently, when your father was trimming my pubes and making jokes about the volume of hair he had to slash through. Have you ever seen those documentaries of Amazonian tribes hacking away at the dense, impenetrable jungle with only machetes and their own will to survive? It was like that. I started laughing and then I started to pee all over his hands. That's real love. I hope you can find somebody that you can be that intimate with, someone who will trim your huge bush (you do have my genes) and make you laugh that hard. In fact, your father also assists me in removing gray hairs from my head. While he uses my tweezers to pluck them, he always smiles and says, "I really love doing this. It makes me look forward to us growing old together."

When cars pick us up to go to the airport, drivers who don't know who I am will often call Daddy "Mr. Wong." They engage with him mostly, ask him the best way to get to the airport, and look to him for instructions on what to do with the luggage. The same happens at hotels and restaurants. People who don't know who I am always assume I took his last name. And it never bothers your father—he always says afterward that he's proud to be Mr. Wong.

And whenever he does, I feel so lucky that I trapped him.

CHAPTER 9

A Guide to Asian Restaurants

D ear Girls,

In case I die suddenly, this is very important information I want to pass down to you, more crucial than money or love. This might be the most important lesson in this book. Being able to select a great Asian restaurant is a *big* source of pride for me. It's what our family does together on the weekends. Life is too short to be wasting meals on bad food, and I would feel deep shame if I ever caught one of you eating at a gross Asian restaurant. I'd rather catch you trafficking cocaine into Thailand in any number of orifices than see you eating at a P. F. Chang's. General rule of thumb: 99 percent of the clientele should be Asian. If you see groups of old Asian women there, that's a very, very good sign.

CUISINE	GOOD SIGNS	BAD SIGNS
VIETNAMESE	• Opens at seven A.M.; closes at eight P.M. • The back of the menu features advertisements for local dentists, lawyers, and real estate agents. • All the employees wear open-toed shoes. • There's a Buddha by the cash register. • There are red fake candles with incense burning. • Waiters have long fingernails that may touch your food and that's okay. • Cash only. • The name has a number in it (yes, I know this is already in *Baby Cobra* but it's important, dammit!).	• Customers are eating pho with a fork. • The waiters are white. • They take American Express. • They don't serve tripe or tendon. • They serve chicken breast. • The name is some unfunny punny bullshit like "Pho Gettaboutit" or "What the Pho."
CHINESE	• There's a tank full of live fish in front. • The waiters rock a maroon bow tie and vest. • The bathroom has pearly pink opaque soap. • It's loud. • Besides water, they serve Hennessy, imitation apple cider, and that's pretty much it. • The pork and shrimp will arrive right away, but it takes an hour to get a glass of water.	• There's truffle oil in the dim sum. • The dim sum is being served on trays. • The waitstaff ask you "How's everything going?" and says things like "Thank you," "Nice to see you," or "Did you leave room for dessert?"

CUISINE	GOOD SIGNS	BAD SIGNS
JAPANESE	• Jazz is playing in the background. • Japanese people singing covers of American songs is playing in the background. • The toilet has a Toto Washlet bidet. • There are strict rules on when to use soy sauce. • There is mochi for dessert (not mochi ice cream).	• Hip-hop is playing in the background. • They serve fake crab. • It's located in Malibu. • Drake eats there. • I'm not going to name the place that I'm really talking about because I don't want the Malibu yakuza coming after my head. • They add twenty ingredients to a piece of sashimi. • The owners are Chinese or Korean.
KOREAN	• The waitresses cut your food with scissors without asking for your permission. • There's a greasy wall full of pictures of the owner with a bunch of Korean celebrities you don't recognize. • You need a Korean friend who speaks Korean to order for you and get the extra banchan. • The chopsticks and rice bowls are metal. • The waitresses feel entitled to pick up your baby and squeeze it. • The windows have newspaper on them.	• The steamed egg in the banchan is not a gray color.
FILIPINO	• It's an auntie's or a lola's house.	• It's a business and not a family member's house.

CHAPTER 10

Bringing Up Bébés

Dear Girls,
Even before you were both born, I put a lot of pressure on myself to be the perfect mom. I used to have so much resentment toward my own mother for not making my needs more of a priority. While most Asian mothers were known to be Tiger Moms, mine was more of a Koala Mom. (You've seen plenty of koalas at the San Diego zoo. They're not fierce like tigers because they're too busy chilling out.) She was never involved in my schoolwork, she sat me in front of the TV to watch the soap opera *All My Children* when I was four years old, and she thought the complaint "I'm bored" was the most spoiled, privileged thing a child could say. When my brother, as a teenager, confessed, "I'm depressed," my mom clapped her hands in front of his face and screamed, "SNAP OUT OF IT!"—which, it turns out, doesn't do shit for depression. Otherwise we'd all be clapping

our hands in front of our faces all day. I always told myself that I would do my best to keep my children stimulated and be more compassionate whenever they were expressing emotion.

In elementary school, my mother would pick me up from after-school care and drive an hour and a half out of San Francisco to take me to the nearest Loehmann's, which is a high-end version of Ross Dress for Less, and also a black hole for middle-aged women. I'm sure it will still exist whenever you read this—because, like the caretaker in *The Shining*, it has *always* existed. When I wasn't being forced to sit in the communal dressing rooms where I had to witness women who, naked, looked like characters from *The Far Side* comics, squeeze themselves into the sausage casing of seven-year-old Dana Buchman and Donna Karan clothes, I was collecting fallen sequins from the floor on my hands and knees. I found it very therapeutic and a nice distraction from all the nude moms hoping to score some happiness and escape in these discount deals. Sometimes my mother would spend two hours there and then reward me for my patience with a cherry Slurpee from the local drugstore. I told myself that I would never take my girls shopping or to run other boring errands with me unless they were old enough to be interested in the clothes.

In elementary school, I constantly had head lice because my mother never bathed me or combed my hair. I thought it was normal since all of my other friends had lice, but realized later that the reason they all had lice was because I gave it to them. I was patient zero. My Jungle Asian mom thought it was perfectly normal, since she grew up with leeches in her backyard pond and had constant head lice in Vietnam. She would scroll through my head with her fingers, pluck out the live lice bugs, and we'd both watch with great pleasure as she'd smash them in between her thumbnails. Blood would squirt out of the lice bugs' bodies and I'd squeal with excitement. My parents' friends all commented that I was a pensive child, but I'm now pretty sure it was just because I was always scratching my head. So I told myself that I would also bathe my children on a regular basis.

My mom always brags that she never kept me to a nap schedule, let me eat what I wanted, avoided helping me with homework, and fed me formula. Then she always concludes, "Look, you turned out fine."

But *I'm not fine*.

I have rosacea, insomnia, and a terrible habit of always assuming the worst when somebody unexpectedly knocks at the door. I panic and think, *If I open that door the bad man is going to stab me in the eye, fill my body with sawdust, and turn me into a giant flesh puppet that he can make dance and sing like one of those goats in* The Sound of Music. Whenever I feel any sort of pain in my body, I assume it's stage-four bone cancer and have an internal debate about whether I'm willing to amputate my foot or not.

All of this made me determined to be a better mom. While I was pregnant, I read this book called *Bringing Up Bébé* about French parenting. It made American parenting seem so unnatural and full of processed food. The logic seemed simple enough: French kids don't snack and that's why they're not picky eaters. When it comes to mealtime, they're actually hungry and will eat whatever is in front of them. French kids don't throw food because, again, they're hungry and know to respect food. My dear friend Aileen, who was a mother of three before I became a mother of one, saw that book lying on my nightstand while I was pregnant. She said, "Oh, you're reading that book of lies," and told me with great certainty, "You *will* feed your kids mac and cheese." I thought, *Wrong—I will*

be the kind of mom who prioritizes whole foods, and I will feed
my children braised leeks and fish and butternut squash.

Then I became a mom, and I realized that *Bringing Up*
Bébé was indeed a bunch of lies.

When Mari started eating solids, I tried to deprive her of
snacks and she still threw my sautéed zucchini on the floor.
That shit only works if you live in a society where everyone
else is eating fennel from the backyard at set mealtimes. But
once Mari saw other children eating goldfish and gummies at
the park, I was finished. She'd beg them to share their snacks
with her and their parents gave me an annoyed, keep-your-
snack-panhandling-baby-away-from-us vibe. I kept trying to
convince her that baby carrots were just as exciting, which is
an almost impossible task. Baby carrots are great, but only
compared to regular carrots or rocks. Mari would smack the
baggie out of my hand and give me a look that said, *Bitch,*
quit trynna fool me. Like Aileen had predicted, I gave in to
mac and cheese before Mari turned one.

The best word to describe parenting is "relentless." It's a
tennis-ball-launcher machine of tasks and mind puzzles and
compromises and poo and pee and spit and barf with un-
limited balls loaded. It's always *something.* The tire pressure
for the minivan is low so somebody needs to Yelp a place that
will help this woman-child learn how to put air in her tires.
We hear rodents scurrying in the attic so now we have to call
the home warranty to call an inferior pest control company
and still pay seventy-five dollars to trap the rat family so they
don't bite our human family. There's no more toilet paper.
There's no more milk. There's no more floss so now I have to
use a strand of my hair to get that piece of chicken out from
between my molars. My sisters are fighting and want to vent
to me about it for an hour each, at least. But I have to go

because now Nikki has a fever and is crying. Mari has a cut that's not getting better. We have to go to the doctor for a second flu shot, this time for Nikki, but it's already almost the end of flu season and she has a fever so she can't get the shot anyway. Fuck, I forgot to pay the water bill. Somebody needs to shred the pile of Bed Bath & Beyond coupons sent to us with our address and names on there. What are the kids going to eat tonight? Ah, shit, the goddamn cottage cheese is expired. I think I got whatever Nikki has and now I have a fever, I have to go lie down. Fuck, now Mari is up with a fever, but is it from Nikki or is that cut really infected? Nobody here is qualified to decide if we need to go to the hospital. I really don't want to go to the hospital. None of my friends that are doctors, pharmacists, or dentists are calling me back. Where are the AA batteries? The crab bouncy exersaucer that I depend on to entertain Nikki so I can eat and breathe is out of batteries. WHERE ARE THE FUCKING BATTERIES? Fuck, I forgot that Father's Day is tomorrow. Maybe I'll just have the kids draw a bunch of squiggles on a card for him. They're too sick to do anything, I'll just draw it like they would and say it's from them. Now the toilet is broken for some reason. Mari might've done that thing where she tries to flush the adult toilet by herself but doesn't have the real torque to fully press down and hold it down for the appropriate time, so she just pushed on it halfway and now the handle is all loose and dangly. Is "dangly" a word? The toilet is overflowing! Nikki is crying hysterically but I have to deal with the toilet, where is the pacifier. WHERE THE FUCK IS THE PACIFIER? Now we have to schedule a parent-teacher conference but I am out of town that week; I'll see if I can switch things. OMG nobody has checked the mail in a week. Now a collections agency is trying to get payment for some doctor visit that nobody remembers going to and that I am pretty sure I paid for already anyway, but I can't remember, and I don't have time to scroll through every expense trying to find it. Can someone please look through all of our payments for the past six months to see if one resembles it? Daddy just found one, but it's like eighty cents less than the number on the collections bill. WHY? Keep looking, maybe it was a different one. Shit, I now realize I never received that new car seat I ordered on Amazon. I have to remember to ask Daddy to look at the cameras and see if someone stole the package off our porch. SOME MOTHER-FUCKER STOLE THAT OFF OUR PORCH! There's video footage of it! Is there a detective we can hire for like half the price of the car seat, to hunt down this thief!?

I had a plan to read to Mari constantly, because someone forwarded me an article threatening that if your child doesn't hear five thousand words by the age of one, they're definitely gonna turn into a prostitute. And even worse, an *illiterate* prostitute. So then I began to read Mari all those "first words" baby board books that didn't have any plot. No beginning, no middle, no story arc. A lot of them would just go like this: Banana, boy, spoon, egg, everybody takes a bath. The End. Finally my mind got so numb from reading all of these dumbass baby books that I said to myself, "Fuck it, no more reading to the baby."

By the time Mari was five months old, at the end of any day, if I held my finger under her nose and felt breath, I was a great mommy.

————

No one tells you how utterly disgusting motherhood is. On our first outing as a family of four, Daddy and I took you both to the Huntington Botanical Gardens in San Marino. The admission is twenty-nine dollars, which is the price of thirteen hamburgers at In-N-Out. But when you have a newborn, your cheapness goes out the window because you're willing to spend any money necessary to save your sanity. That day, we absolutely needed to get the fuck out of the house.

Nikki was only four weeks old, which meant I still had afterbirth leaking out of my pussy. In my preparation to ensure we had enough diapers, wipes, snacks, and extra outfits, I neglected to pack extra breast pads and pantyliners for myself. So my pantyliner quickly became soaked with old, brown blood, and the adhesive became not so adhesive. We were admiring the bonsai in the Japanese garden when I felt the pantyliner sliding out of my underwear. I rushed to the bathroom where there was a long line of Asian senior citizens in giant hats and Uniqlo ultra-light down jackets, prepping themselves for their morning group tai chi exercises. While waiting, my right boob began to throb painfully. I knew what was coming. I cupped my hand on my breast and in addition to being rock hard, my dress was soaking wet from the leaking milk. I pulled my dress to look down, and my boob was all veiny and looked like a close-up of somebody's pulsating eyeball. If I didn't empty my breast soon, I knew this could lead to a clogged duct and even worse, mastitis, which is an infection that causes a fever. One of my poor girlfriends got it and was on antibiotics for a month. Her pus-filled lump had grown to the size of a softball and had to be drained all the time.

I rushed back to you girls and Daddy, who were now in a field lined with naked marble statues. I grabbed Nikki out of her sleep and made her latch on to my breast, hoping she'd drain it right away. Flies and mosquitoes from the garden were gathering at my legs as she ate, and the afterbirth juice just continued to gush out and now soak the butt area of my dress, giving my already milk-soaked outfit an additional, sophisticated, bleeding-out-of-my-asshole look. Meanwhile Mari was rolling around in the park's fertilizer and Daddy was chasing her, trying to get her to stop while fishing tiny branches and rocks out of her mouth. Nikki took a break from my nipple to stare into my eyes and have an explosive up-the-back poo-poo. As I sat her up to pat her back and burp her, she spit up all the milk she just drank onto my dress. My striped Topshop outfit was now fully a towel—full of spit up, poo-poo, milk, and uterine lining. More flies and mosquitoes gathered. I could see other pedestrians passing by in the garden, sniffing the air, wondering if that smell was fertilizer, me, or a dead body hidden in the garden.

When we returned to the parking lot, a man with a Bernie Sanders sticker on his Volkswagen Beetle pulled up next to our van and asked, "Are you leaving?" Gesturing to our giant double stroller and all the bags of snacks and supplies underneath it, I replied, "Yes, but it's going to take us a couple minutes." The driver, in his Grateful Dead shirt and beard, said, "Well, hurry up." And then me, in my dress heavy and drenched with all of these bodily fluids, tired, fed up, sincerely asked my standard question: "Are you kidding me?"

"Yeah," he said. "You're not the only person in the world."

I don't remember what really happened from there. I kind of went black, like I had on that plane with Mari, and vaguely remember screaming things like:

"You're a fucking piece of shit!"

"I hope you get kicked out of your local co-op!"

"No wonder you're coming to this garden all by yourself!

Your children must hate you! Why don't you suck the
1 percent top of my dick?!"

And then that asshole yelled, "Fuck you!" and drove away
while your father ran after his car, screaming all sorts of terrible ways he was hoping the man would die. "I hope you die,
you fuck! I hope you get stung by a thousand bees, and your
glasses fall off and you die like Macaulay Culkin in *My Girl,*
you Phish-listening fuck!"

I don't think your father and I have ever felt as connected
as we did that day.

Because motherhood is disgusting, you spend so much
energy cleaning up that you're left with no time for yourself.
So I gave in to TV pretty fast. When Mari turned one, *Moana*
was very popular. Thank God it wasn't *Frozen*. *Moana* is
every feminist Asian American Pacific Islander's dream. She
doesn't have a love story and is a strong-ass curious chief,
providing for her people. And those songs are *the shit*. We
also showed Mari a lot of Hayao Miyazaki films, like *Ponyo*
and *My Neighbor Totoro*. I tried to stay away from the classic
Disney princess movies. In addition to featuring a lot of un-
empowered women, those movies are just so white. White
people and stories about white people are not bad, it's just
that when you live in America, everything is so inherently
white. I don't want you to grow up wishing you were white
and having that inform all of your decisions later on in life. I
want you to be proud of having black hair and Asian features.

Still, you can't deny that, like goldfish and gummies, *The
Little Mermaid* is fucking magical. I still feel sparkles in my
stomach when I watch it. Despite Ariel wearing an ocean bra
for most of that movie, and despite the fact that a man ultimately saves her from an evil plus-sized sea witch, and despite

Ariel ditching her entire family for this man just because he's a handsome prince, I gave in and showed *The Little Mermaid* to Mari on repeat. Those songs are also *the shit*. I'm a sucker for a drunk seagull best friend and since this is a safe space free of judgment: Ariel's dad is kinda hot? I still find my feelings about King Triton confusing. He looks like Santa with abs and a tail.

————

Once I had Mari, all I wanted was my own damn mommy. I quickly let go of all that unnecessary resentment toward her. She came to L.A. whenever I asked and was so helpful. After parents welcome a newborn, most visitors come to just hold the baby while it's sleeping. *Nobody* needs to hold the baby while it's sleeping. It's basically the only time you *don't* need to hold the baby. But when my mom stayed, she'd change diapers, scrub the poo out of clothes and sheets, cook and wash all the dishes, and soothe Mari while she was fussy. She drove to Costco to get us toilet paper, groceries, batteries, and always made sure to fill up my car with gas. It was amazing.

And then Nikki was born two years after Mari, and my mom returned to Los Angeles to stay with Mari while we were in the hospital. Shortly after my C-section, Mommy and Daddy both ate some bad Chinese food. (We should have known better. The waitstaff asked us, "How are you doing today?" Bad sign.) At exactly six P.M. I started having frothy diarrhea and called to Daddy from the toilet, "Please grab Nikki!" who I could hear crying from our bedroom. He shouted back, "I'm throwing up!" He then came into the bathroom to see how I was doing, and saw me with my panties at my ankles, throwing up into the sink. He started laughing, which made me laugh, and my body continued to betray me as I peed all over the floor.

While Daddy and I were curled up in fetal positions, moaning in our bed, my mom cleaned up all my barf out of the sink, wiped my piss, and held buckets under our mouths. She took care of Nikki at night, when Nikki was waking up every two hours to eat. My mom would prepare her bottle and then change her diaper. It was even more amazing. She was like a Vietnamese Mary Poppins. I take that back. My mom would hate it if I called her that. She doesn't believe in sugarcoating things and she would never feed any birds. When we were recently watching *Mary Poppins Returns* with Emily Blunt, my mom said, "That lady is really silly."

"Who, Emily Blunt?" I asked. "Why? She married that fine-ass man from *The Office* who became Jack Ryan."

"No, Mary Poppins."

"What are you talking about? Mary Poppins is magical."

"She's unrealistic."

"Well, it's a kids' movie."

"She can fly and speed travel—"

"You mean teleport."

"She uses her superpowers to nurture other people's kids. She should use them to rob a bank."

She had a good point.

Sure, my mom continued to give me unsolicited advice. She kept on telling me to just give the baby a bottle of formula instead of breastfeeding. She told me I was too uptight about the baby looking at the TV and showed Mari unofficial YouTube *Boss Baby* videos when I specifically asked her not to. She called my house a dirty hippie commune (there are a lot of singing bowls and essential oils). She constantly criticized my spending habits and questioned my every purchase and meal order. But she was *there* for me. So I just didn't care anymore. It made me realize that the most important part of parenting, relationships, pretty much anything—is just actually being there.

My mom was never the type to write me long letters or birthday cards. We never got mani-pedis together, she never gave me a locket with our picture in it. She wouldn't tell me I looked beautiful, help me shop for prom, or soothe me when a boy broke my heart. But she was there. She kept me safe. She did her best to make me tough. She fed me the most delicious home-cooked meals. For lunch, she'd pack me rare sliced steak over white rice and steamed broccoli. She sent me to private school from kindergarten through twelfth grade. She is still there for me. She will always be there for me, as long as she's able. That's a great mom. And she could give two fucks about that French parenting book.

I hope to be half as good a mommy to you as she was to me. I'm not promising that I'll clean up your adult piss and shit, but I promise to do it for your babies at least. Or I'll pay someone else to do it.

CHAPTER 11

Uncle Andrew

Dear Girls,

From kindergarten until eighth grade, I attended an all-girls school called Katherine Delmar Burke. It was tradition for the third-graders to participate in the annual California Pageant, an exciting evening where we didn't have to wear our green uniform jumpers over white blouses. Students dressed up as important historical California figures and gave a small speech about their legacies. But since history is written by men, most important historical figures are men, and a lot of us little girls had to play men. This Filipino-Russian girl was Willie Mays. I don't know why they couldn't have her be Philip Vera Cruz or something, anything at least a little closer. We were all very jealous of the handful of girls who actually got to portray women, and wear fabulous over-the-top costumes that were most likely designed by friends of their well-connected parents. And I, whose parents had no connection to anyone important in San Francisco, played one of history's greatest villains: Richard Nixon. Those few girls wore gowns with long matching gloves, and I got to be the guy who bugged a hotel and whose nickname was Dick.

My parents complained about the cost of the forty-dollar Richard Nixon mask. They didn't understand why the manufacturer of those thin plastic Halloween masks that slice your face when they inevitably crack wouldn't just make their own cheap version of a Richard Nixon mask. Instead they were forced to pay for, in addition to the overpriced private school tuition, a rubber mask of a disgraced president. It was the same one the surfer gang of robbers wore in the movie *Point Break*. So I guess the only good part was that it kind of made me feel a little closer to Keanu.

My brother, your uncle Andrew, figured out how to squeeze a little more value out of the mask. When he was twenty years old and home from college for the holidays, he put it on and dressed up in a vintage plaid suit. He stood in the kitchen, leaned against the pistachio-green refrigerator with his hands casually tucked into the brown-and-orange pockets, and waited for my dad to come home. My dad, already the type of person who was so paranoid of intruders that he never left the garage door open for more than three seconds after pulling in or out, freaked the fuck out when he saw this weirdo in the kitchen. He immediately went for a frying pan and, just as he was about to strike, my brother took the mask off and in between laughs, doubled over, raised a hand, and confessed, "It's me! It's me!"

My dad screamed, "OH FOR GOD'S SAKE, ANDREW!"

I was upset at Andrew for startling my dad and almost giving him a heart attack. Like I said, my dad was much older than all of my friends' parents, and I was constantly scared of him dying. At the same time, I was laughing too. And this is sort of how my attitude has always been toward Andrew, see-sawing between extreme distress and uncontrollable laughter, like a woman in a Victorian mental asylum.

As you girls both already know by the time you read this, your uncle Andrew is, um, a character? Out of his mind? Kooky? A man who has always had a place to sleep but behaves like he's homeless? I grew up feeling like I could be anything because my very own brother was *nothing* like anything that had ever existed before. He was an Asian American boy constantly living somewhere between a music festival, a garage sale, and a nervous breakdown. His walls were lined with shelves of jazz records, hip-hop records, and vintage toys. My favorite was his metal, life-sized chicken that would walk and lay metal eggs. I'd play dress up in his closet, where he had an extensive collection of wigs, props, and used fur coats.

When I was in second grade, Andrew gave me the cassette tape for *Eddie Murphy: Delirious,* which sparked my interest in stand-up comedy. I'd listen to the tape over and over again, and obviously did not understand all the jokes. But I knew it was funny and wrong, and I loved it. Andrew introduced me to *Pee-wee's Playhouse* and Miles Davis and *The Autobiography of Malcolm X* and I loved all of it. Plus, I became the only seven-year-old in my class who could properly use the term "motherfucker." My brother was kind of like a middle school boy and also like a freshman at UC Berkeley in the 1970s.

When I was a freshman in high school I raided Andrew's insane closet for a Halloween costume. A lot of girls were dressing up as schoolgirl Britney Spears or one of the Spice Girls. I chose to be the pimp from the movie *I'm Gonna Git You Sucka,* which at the time I thought was about the funniest movie I'd ever seen. I wore my brother's long, black curly wig topped off with a wide-brimmed hat, plaid flared pants, sparkly orange turtleneck, black sunglasses, platform boots, and a fur coat, and walked around the hallways with a limp, committing to a need for my dad's cane. I smelled like Goodwill but acted like I reeked of money. All of the male upperclassmen thought my costume was very cool while the head of admissions thought letting me, a girl who wanted to dress like a man from the seventies who prided himself on controlling prostitutes, into this prestigious liberal arts school had been a huge mistake.

In college, Andrew got in trouble constantly. He got caught with drugs at the airport. He got caught doing drugs at school. He had long hair down to his butt for the express purpose that people would confuse him with my sister Mimi from the back, which I'm sure was distressing for Mimi, and even more distressing for Mimi's friends who thought they saw her on the street, and then were utterly terrified by the reveal. And for most of his life, he exclusively dated white women. Frumpy white women. Hippie white women. White women with grown-ass kids. Mentally unstable white women. White women white women white women. They all thought he was some sort of rare creature with his long, luxurious, jet-black ponytail, adventurous spirit, and terrible grades. Because he had grown up with three sisters, he was extremely comfortable with how complicated and gross women are. My sisters and I all trained him to be unfazed by dandruff, foot odor, and menstrual-blood-stained panties soaking in the sink. And white women really appreciated that. Asian American women never seemed to take an interest. Whatever quality in Andrew white women valued as "exotic," Asian American women deemed "disturbingly weird."

Growing up, I thought he and my siblings were the coolest people in the world. They took me out on dates with their boyfriends and girlfriends. On our family road trips to Monterey Bay or Los Angeles, they'd stack up all the suitcases in the back of the Volvo station wagon and put blankets on top to make a luxurious queen-sized mobile-home bed for me while the three of them sat in the back. If anyone had rear-ended us I would have flown directly through the front windshield but that's basically every car ride for a child born before 1985. Those are some of my best memories. Me and all of my siblings together in one car with my parents, eating McDonald's hash browns and listening to them banter with Joan Baez playing in the background.

Both of my sisters, Mimi and Julia, had attended the same all-girls K–8 school, Katherine Delmar Burke, before me. When I was there, teachers still talked about how Julia, my oldest sibling, was such a prodigy at impressionism at the age of twelve. She had painted a beautiful portrait of a melancholy woman in a white hat onto a stool, like a Joni Mitchell album cover you could sit on, and I did sit on it, proudly, every single day during art class. My other sister, Mimi, was known for being an incredible athlete. She was great at basketball, soccer, *and* volleyball. It's shocking that my parents didn't know she was gay. She was also extremely talented in metal shop. Again, shocking that, in addition to the knee brace she always wore and her huge collection of mountain bikes and drill bits, they couldn't see all of the telltale signs that she much preferred pussy. Like Julia, Mimi also was a great artist. In high school, Mimi had made a beautiful stained glass window of a faceless Chinese woman dressed in green, playing the flute. It still sits in my mom's living room today, and I will probably fight Mimi for it when my mom dies, even though Mimi was the one who made it. I hope to pass that faceless Chinese flute woman down to you girls. I'm trying to strategize right now how I can convince Mimi's son that you two will need and deserve it more. Maybe I'll just say, "Hashtag time's up!" over and over even though it does not really apply.

My brother had a reputation for being super cool and popular, but he was also known for getting in a shitload of trouble. Looking back, I'm grateful that the one son in my family was not aspirational. It really freed me to do whatever I wanted. He didn't trap me into any sort of success paradigm; whatever expectations that had existed crumbled long before I was born and that allowed me to make my own way. My parents didn't tell me what to do or how to live because they were so occupied with the slow process of giving up on my brother. For example, I hated piano so much that I quit when I was in second grade. For most Chinese people, that's like getting divorced after one week of marriage and a huge, expensive wedding. At my last recital ever, I played two notes of some boring-ass classical song and then just stopped, because I hadn't practiced or learned it. But I still had the nerve to bow at the end, to confused and slow applause. When I returned to sit in between my parents to hear the rest of Mrs. Butler's students actually play their songs instead of just flaunting their parents' wasted money like I had, my mom and dad didn't seem embarrassed at all. They simply did not care. They just sat through the rest of the performances, and my dad, always tired from his long and late hours at the hospital, fell asleep. On the car ride home, I said, "I wanna stop piano." Instead of chastising me, my dad just said calmly, "Okay, Alexandra. That's your choice."

When I was in eighth grade, Mimi came out of the closet. My mom thought it was a phase and that she was just being seduced by lesbianism the way she'd been seduced by sports and metal shop and not shaving her legs or armpits. How on earth could her tallest, most beautiful daughter (with the second most luxurious ponytail after Andrew) be gay? Why would God do that to her? Soon after telling us she had a girlfriend, Mimi chopped off all her long hair, tired of people assuming that she was straight or Andrew. When I greeted her at the door, she asked me to go upstairs and tell my mother, so that my mother wouldn't have a heart attack and die upon seeing my sister's new Asian k.d. lang cut without warning. My mom couldn't hide her disappointment, and then tried to be positive by expressing how great it was that hair grew so that Mimi could go back to being pretty and normal. She very openly hoped Mimi would one day get back together with her high school boyfriend, Nigel. Ten years later, Mimi arrived to a family dinner at our favorite restaurant, Ming River, with some news:

"Sorry I'm late. I just saw Nigel," said Mimi.

My mom's eyes lit up. "Oh really?! Wow, how does he—"

Mimi: "It was nice to see him, Mom. He got married a couple of years ago and has a baby now."

My mother's face fell as she said "oh" again, but not with the same excited surprise. Then she cried into a pink cloth napkin at the large round table for ten minutes, mourning the loss of her delusion that her daughter would eventually return to the D.

Because of my siblings, my parents did not prioritize academics and were more focused on keeping me alive and not depressed. Andrew had been diagnosed with manic-depressive disorder when he was in high school. Mimi had a tragic accident in college, when she went hiking and fell down a deep hole. She was stuck there overnight and had to get helicoptered out. At the local hospital they stitched up her leg without cleaning it thoroughly, and she got an intense infection and almost had to have her leg amputated. My siblings taught me that you could recover from failure. Julia was always so good at everything. She was great at piano, painting, and academia. She got into Harvard Law School and my mother told everyone and their mothers. But then Julia dropped out her first year. After that, Julia was very down on herself and seemed lost in her life. When I offered her some of my Flintstones chewable vitamins, she replied, "I don't deserve to eat vitamins." She tried cooking, teaching, and being a camp leader at my youth center while I went there, which was annoying. But she finally went on to get her medical degree and become a great pediatrician. Now she's not practicing but is very fulfilled being focused on her kids. She's right where she should be.

So by the time I came around, my parents were just happy if all their kids kept their limbs and weren't emotionally stuck in the sunken place.

The movie *High Fidelity* came out when I was a junior in high school. John Cusack's character goes through five different relationships. The statistics teacher asked us how we felt about it. Everyone except for me said they found it depressing. They all thought they were going to marry their high school sweethearts (so naïve!). Older people know that you have to go through multiple relationships to find the right one. You both will probably go through three to five serious relationships in your life before finding your person, if you're even lucky enough. Older people found the movie relatable and uplifting because even though John Cusack's character doesn't end up getting married, he does end up in a relationship with a woman where he can be comfortable and be himself. But I didn't have to see *High Fidelity* to know this was true. I had witnessed it all through my siblings.

————

Andrew went to China for two years after college and returned as an extremely serious person. He grew up going to private school and made no Chinese American friends, and then spent two years surrounded by all Chinese people. There, Andrew studied acupuncture and backpacked through rural provinces. Your father's theory is that Andrew became possessed by the spirit of a poor, old Chinese man who has not left his body since.

When he returned to the United States, he behaved like there was an impending war that we needed to hunt and gather for. At the end of any meal, he'd ask to eat the unfinished food on our plates. Sometimes he'd not just ask family, but friends or guests of the family who were also sitting at the table. He came down on me for acting so ungratefully toward our parents' constant sacrifice and lamented how badly he had behaved in his youth.

All of a sudden, he'd inherited the extreme immigrant paranoia that everyone is out to get you. When my parents would go on vacation, my brother would blast classical music, turn on all the lights, and place stuffed animals in the windows. Like Kevin McCallister from *Home Alone,* he hoped potential thieves would be fooled by the silhouettes. He didn't seem to realize that Kevin McCallister used human-shaped mannequins and had them *move around*. Andrew was betting on robbers being deterred by frozen outlines of my childhood Popples and Glo Worms. Then again, if I saw a grown man playing with stuffies while blasting a Wagner symphony, I certainly wouldn't want to fuck with him.

To save money on food and shelter, he lived at home until he was thirty-five. He avoided paying rent the way I avoid paying for online shipping (even if it means putting a ten-dollar pair of undies that reads BOSS BITCH on the butt in my cart to bring my purchase over the fifty-dollar finish line). This is not uncommon for a lot of Asian American men, especially in San Francisco, where rent has been rising exponentially. They don't so much love their moms as they love not paying rent. They are so afraid of spending money that they live at home until they get married. And no cooking can compare to their mothers'. "Free" is the secret ingredient that makes every meal extra delicious. The filial piety is transformed into arrested development. Never marry these men. This is where being with someone of your own race can backfire. You will always be in competition with your mother-in-law. Andrew is still not even fully moved out. He occupies several closets at our mom's house, filled with artifacts from his various hoarding hobbies and get-rich-quick resale schemes. The profit margin on some of these resales was as little as twenty cents. His first one was records, just because he had thousands of them in his room and hidden in the fireplace. A person would have to live for a million years and never sleep to listen to all of my brother's records from start to finish. My mom threatened to put them in a pile and burn them if he didn't get them out of her house. But once he purged all the records, he moved on to collecting free books and reselling them on eBay. Then it was vacuum cleaners, orchids, rugs, and worm juice (ask him what that is, I really don't know). His current obsession is cars. Every once in a while he'll show up in Los Angeles and use our house as a pee-pee stop after picking up a '97 Buick LeSabre he bought off Craigslist from Rancho Cucamonga.

But all of his hoarding has come in handy. For my baby shower, Andrew packed and drove a U-Haul of old baby gear, clothes, and books from him and my sisters. Sure, half of the books were from Goodwill and caked with furry mold. But the other half were great and both of you girls loved them. He planted all of the succulents in our backyard (they used to be in other people's front yards before he stole pieces of them—thank you, Uncle Andrew!).

Whenever he comes to visit the house, he dilutes our soaps, installs gutters that only cause more problems, caulks stuff, de-caulks other stuff, and does it all without asking. He has lots of good intentions with poor execution. He's like an eccentric, self-taught handyman that just kind of comes over and does things on his own. Sort of like Tim Allen's character on *Home Improvement,* if he wasn't trained at all and used to rock a sweet ponytail.

His daughter, my niece and your cousin, had been begging for a dog as long as she could speak. One day, Andrew called me to ask if he could come over. I assumed he had bought another 1984 Lexus in Calabasas off Craigslist and wanted to take a shit at our house and refill his Dasani water bottle before the long drive back to San Francisco where he could sell the car to make eighteen dollars. Instead, he came over with a dog named Astrid.

My niece had made it clear she wanted a puppy and Andrew's wife made it even more clear that she wanted a small dog. Astrid was neither. But she did possess a very significant quality to Andrew: She was free. She had fled the 2018 Malibu fires and nobody could identify her owner. Andrew rescued her from a kill center where she was about to get euthanized. He didn't know anything about how to take care of a dog and treated the adoption of this pet like he had won a goldfish at the local fair. He didn't read anything online or ask my sister Mimi, a very seasoned dog owner, any questions. At Christmas, when we were all spending time at Mimi's apartment in San Francisco, Mimi reminded him to never leave Astrid in her backyard alone. Andrew thought Mimi was just being anal and precious about her garden, and wanted him to simply keep a tight surveillance if Astrid pooed anywhere. All of a sudden, we heard Andrew screaming, "Heel, Astrid! Heel!" And a huge raccoon was on top of Astrid. It bit a hole through her ear and scratched underneath her eye. Andrew did not understand that a backyard is like a prison yard for animals.

My niece wept and was super angry at her dad for leaving Astrid out there by herself. I explained to her that taking care of a dog is a big deal, and kind of like having a new baby for the first time. I told her that her dad couldn't possibly be expected to know everything, and tried to make her feel less bad about my neglectful brother. I said, "When I was a new parent, I left Mari sleeping in the middle of our queen-sized bed. At the time, she had never rolled over, so I assumed it was safe to leave her there while I went to the bathroom. As I was flushing, I heard a *plop* and then found Mari facedown on our bamboo floor, wide awake and hysterically crying. Luckily no bones were broken but that was a big lesson I had to learn. And I never left her or Nikki sleeping on an open bed again." Then my niece looked at me like I was way worse than Andrew.

Despite all of his crazy, my brother has always been deeply loyal to my family. He inherited my father's extremely non–Asian American quality of giving zero fucks about saving face. My brother idolized my dad so much and was absolutely devastated when he passed away. He hosted the funeral and just kept speaking way over his designated time, to the point where our minister had to intervene and ask him to stop talking. When someone that my dad hated unexpectedly showed up to the funeral, my sisters and I didn't know what to do. My father had refused to speak to her for years. On the microphone in front of a hundred attendees, my brother looked at her and said, "You have to leave. You have to leave right now. We can have our own relationship, but my father never liked you and specifically said that if you were to ever attend his funeral, to have henchmen pick you up and carry you out." After she refused to leave, my brother's two very tall friends from growing up escorted her out. Right after, I told my dad in his casket that he would've loved what had just transpired. I said, "Dad, you would've laughed your head off. Andrew just kicked you-know-who out of your funeral in your honor! With henchmen! You would be so proud!"

And since my dad passed away, my brother has been a companion to my mom. He picks her up from the airport. He goes with her to weddings. When I was performing in San Francisco, he insisted on driving me to and from all my shows.

So even though I told you to never marry a man like him, don't judge a book by its cover. Just because he's bald and cheap doesn't mean he's not a good man. He allowed all of his siblings to fail because he had failed so frequently and so hugely. When you're the only son, there's a ton of pressure to be something great. And all that pressure turned him into a super fucking weird, crazy diamond.

I often now accidentally call my brother by your dad's name. I know it's gross and strange, but I think it's because they're the two men I feel most comfortable being a complete cunt in front of. I can tell Andrew to put the tricycle back in the garage without having to say please, and I love that. So I apologize for not giving you girls your own brother, because having a brother like Andrew has been such a special part of my life. My mother wasn't as overprotective of me because of him. Sisters are great for being close to and having a friend and gossip partner. But my brother will always be one of my best friends, a person that I can trust to take care of and protect me. He's a man who does things for me when I don't even have to ask, even if he does them unbelievably wrong. (Andrew, when you read this, the sink in the guest room is clogged again.)

CHAPTER 12

My Least Favorite Question

Dear Girls,

A question I always get asked is: "What is it like being an Asian American woman in Hollywood?" I hate this question almost as much as I hate "What's it like to be a female in comedy?" because nobody wants their identity and defining characteristics reduced to just race and gender. I resent that white men never get asked, "What is it like to be a white man in movies?" And what disappoints me even more is that the people asking me are always Asian American. It feels like they want to hear a titillating story about a meeting with a high-powered Hollywood executive, who sat me down in his office and said, "Look, we love you, Ali. In fact . . . we *love you long time!*" then threw rice in my face, forced me to watch Mickey Rooney's scene from *Breakfast at Tiffany's* on a loop for forty-eight hours straight, and kicked me out of his office screaming, "You'll never make it in the white man's world, you chinky ho! DU-NUH-NUH-NUH-NUH-NUH-NUH-NAAAAAAAH!" (That, unfortunately, has never happened to me.) Aspiring Asian American writers and performers never seem to inquire about what I think are more important and interesting topics like:

How do you overcome failure?

How do you write a good joke?

How do you learn to live life on the road?

How do you choose who to collaborate with?

How do you stay safe?

The answers to making it, to me, are a lot more universal than anyone's race or gender, and center on having a tolerance for delayed gratification, a passion for the craft, and a willingness to fail. But it's the number one question on their minds, because most people, including myself, are conditioned to define other people via race and gender. So much so that, whenever a friend lets me know they're dating somebody new, my first question is: "What race are they?" The answer is always: "He's a white man, Ali, okay? Why do you always ask me that?!" And my response is always to raise my eyebrows and stare into my poke bowl.

And yes, there have been and are still many times these days when I have to check people for defining me via my race and gender. For my recent stand-up dates in Las Vegas, the promoters put together clips of my jokes to play on the radio as commercials. I sat in my office listening to their selection for approval. From *Hard Knock Wife*, they chose an abridged version of the bit where I talk about nannies:

"If you are hiring a twenty-five-year-old pretty young thing to be your nanny, you a dumbass. If we had hired a twenty-five-year-old man, you best believe that I would eat the shit out of his butthole." Now of course, you cannot say "shit" or "butthole" on the radio. So in place of those words, they used what they felt was a very appropriate sound effect: a gong. When I heard that, I put my head into my hands in disappointment. I replied to the promoters: "Please take out that gong. Give me a regular beep like you would give to literally ANY OTHER COMEDIAN." I mean seriously, would they ever even consider doing that to anyone else? "All right, we got George Lopez coming to town. Cue up 'La Cucaracha.'"

Over the past three years, I have had to do a ton of press. One local reporter was a sixty-year-old white man with an Asian wife who was way too excited to tell me that he had an Asian wife. He spent every third sentence telling me about Anna Maria Luisa. He kept drawing connections between my work and his Filipino wife's family. Some of them didn't make sense, and some of them were kind of a stretch. "I noticed that food is a huge theme for you. In my wife's family, food is so important. Lola [this is a Filipino word for "grandma," which he made sure to over-pronounce to the point where I thought a grandma from Guadalajara possessed his hairy porcelain body for a second] always insists that we eat before going out for the afternoon." That's not necessarily an Asian thing. To me it sounds like Grandma is encouraging people to eat lunch. All sorts of people around the world eat lunch. People in Egypt eat lunch. Black people eat lunch. Termites eat lunch. All of these generalizations he was making about Asian culture, all this authority he was asserting over Asian culture, were really fucking annoying. I was excited to talk about my work process and instead all he wanted to discuss was how his Filipino mother-in-law made delicious shrimp, how he was scared of shrimp before being married to a Filipino, and many other observations about Filipinos and shrimp.

———

I was lucky enough to grow up in San Francisco. It's a beautiful city with a fantastic bridge. It's also *full* of Asian people. And I went to UCLA, which is also known as the

University of
Caucasians
Lost
Among Asians.

UCLA was like Asian Wakanda phase two. Yes, there were a lot of Asian American students who were studying to be doctors and lawyers. But I also saw Asian American people undertaking extremely artistic and creative endeavors. I had friends in the design program and others who played jazz. I saw Filipino students performing impressive hip-hop dance routines and traditional stick fighting. I was semi-obsessed with this one Asian American punk girl who had bleached blond hair and piercings all over her face. (Asian punk girl—if you happen to be reading this book, I hope you know I thought you were awesome and always wanted to get to know you! Please DM me. Hopefully, by the time you do, my husband might give me permission to go outside of the marriage, as long as it's with a woman.) One Japanese American girl in the film program made the most beautiful stop-motion video of these naked, clay human beings making love and melting into each other and then becoming new people afterward. It was disturbing, sexy, beautiful, and scary all at once—like a Jennifer Lopez movie. And it was very important for me to know, early on in my life, that an Asian American woman was capable of making all of those complicated emotions cohabitate in one amazing art piece.

My dad had such overwhelming pride in the accomplishments of other Asian Americans that he always made sure to be aware of what any high-profile Asian Americans were doing. When Margaret Cho's pilot episode of *All-American Girl*, the first network TV sitcom featuring an Asian American family, aired, my entire family gathered around the kitchen table in excitement to watch on our small kitchen TV. Our refrigerator door was covered with newspaper clippings about Michael Chang, Kristi Yamaguchi, Lou Diamond Phillips, Dante Basco, B. D. Wong, and Tyson Beckford (he's half Chinese). Even though William Hung, an *American Idol* contestant with a thick Chinese accent, and his popularity were a little problematic, my dad still purchased his debut album: *Hung Time*. Or was it *Hung-ry for Love*? (I don't actually remember what it was called, nobody does.) He got famous from doing a cover of "She Bangs" by Ricky Martin, and my dad played it in the living room, while we all seesawed between full grimacing and wild laughing. It was a bewildering time for us all.

Even though my parents were very progressive, and extremely enthusiastic about Asian Americans in the arts, they were not very supportive when I first told them I was moving to NYC to pursue stand-up comedy. When I pointed out that Margaret Cho (who had gone to high school with my oldest sister) was a successful stand-up comedian, and that Maxine Hong Kingston was a very respected writer, my parents said to me, "They are extraordinary exceptions. The chances of all that for you are very slim." It was hurtful but ultimately, given their backgrounds, I understood why they wanted to be practical.

Asians like predictability. We like safety. We want to know that if we work hard, there will be a payoff. Downward mobility and the shame that comes with it is an Asian immigrant nightmare. And in entertainment, you *very* well might not make it despite all of those years you invested. There is no linear path to success, and no linear path to maintaining it even if you do achieve it. But it's important to remember immigrant parents, grandparents, or great-grandparents took the biggest, most unpredictable risk of all: They came to America, when there was no Rosetta Stone, no Google Maps, no blogs, no Airbnb, no cellphones. Some came before there were airplanes or electricity. I could never be that brave and take that kind of risk without all of that. I straight up refuse to go to a restaurant if it's not well reviewed on Yelp. Then again, if our relatives had been able to Yelp America before coming over, they might have thought twice. Those reviews would have been mixed: "The opportunity is on point, but they kind of overdo it with the institutional racism and the guns. 3 stars."

My mom came to the United States when she was twenty years old, by herself, not knowing any English, at the beginning of the Vietnam War. People screamed "gook" and all sorts of other hateful names she couldn't even understand. My dad's dad came to the United States as an eight-year-old boy on a boat, through Angel Island, all by himself. When he was an adult, he chose his overseas Chinese wife from a picture. She, my grandmother, came to the United States in her late teens, not knowing what her future, or even her husband, would be like. What if my grandfather had severe erectile dysfunction like everybody I dated in my twenties? I guess he didn't or they worked around it, because he and my grandmother had three kids together. But imagine not even knowing if your *husband* smells good or appreciates *Game of Thrones*? You would reference how "Winter is Coming" and he'd give you a blank stare like, *What the fuck are you talking about?*

My grandfather passed away when I was eight years old, the exact same age that he was when he came to the United States. His biggest worry when he was eight was how he was going to survive in this strange, new country. My biggest worry when I was eight was if I was going to be Miss Piggy or Paula Abdul for Halloween. I got my first paid job when I was fifteen, at GapKids, folding tiny baby-sized hoodies and taking people's money and giving them receipts and change. My grandfather's first job was working as a live-in cook and house cleaner for a family in Monterey, California. He was, again, *eight years old.* I often think about what it would be like for my grandfather to see me now. What would he think about me saying all of the disgusting things I say onstage? How would he feel about his granddaughter talking about what she lusts after? How I obsess over the most trivial problems. How I make a living by talking about what I want. How people pay to see his granddaughter *just talk.* He'd probably think I was some sort of magician with ancient powers, derived from behaving very well in a past life. Or a witch, I guess. At the very least, he'd definitely have the opposite opinion of all those jealous-ass white male comedians who say things like "People only like your comedy because you're female and a minority." My grandpa would be like, "I can't believe people like your comedy! You're a female *and* a minority!"

And remembering where I came from, and who I came from, has always humbled me and been a constant source of motivation. My father grew up in an apartment with no running water and slept on a twin bed that he shared with his two sisters *and* mother while his father slept on newspaper on the floor. My dad's sisters didn't get to go to college because all the money had to be invested in him—the boy. All of the pressure in the world was on my dad to "make it" for the whole family, and I still can't believe that he rose to the occasion. He studied like an animal, got into UC Berkeley Medical School, and worked his ass off to become a great anesthesiologist. Thinking about how far my grandfather and father came encouraged me immensely. I strove to travel at least some of the distance they had. Because of this, I was never that upset about my living conditions, even when I was sharing an NYC apartment with six other people. I always remembered my grandfather—an eight-year-old child working as a houseboy for a cruel family, sleeping on newspapers in their basement. Like I said, he continued to sleep on newspaper as an adult when he had three children and a wife crammed into that tiny apartment. Is it possible that he just liked sleeping on newspapers so he could catch up on current events while falling asleep? We'll never know. Wish he'd written a *Dear Grandkids* book!

One Asian value that I'm grateful was passed down to me is knowing how to save money. Immigrants are shocked by how expensive everything is when they arrive in this country— *Wait, this bowl of pho costs over fifty cents? The price of this bullshit they call brunch is the same as my father's salary in Vietnam! One meal of eggs and toast . . . equal a month's worth of harvesting rice in the sun?? Tickets to see that pregnant comedian live when she's not even pregnant anymore cost the same as my very dangerous diesel moped!* They never get over that habit of trying to stretch a dollar, which, to their credit, is a very useful survival skill. I was taught to never even order a drink with a meal. My mom would sometimes feed us spoiled food even though my dad was a fucking anesthesiologist. If you shook a jug of soy milk that was clearly turning into tofu, she would say it was still good. It all used to embarrass me and made me feel like I was living in a savings prison. My mom yelled at me when I was two minutes into a shower: "You're taking too long! Get out!" To this day, she only wants me to shower at the gym so I don't waste her water (I also steal menstrual pads for her from Equinox and she doesn't even get her period anymore). Whenever we traveled anywhere, my parents would feign interest in a time-share just to get that free breakfast. If there is only one thing I know for absolute certain in this world, it's this—my parents never had the intention of purchasing a time-share. We grew up in a huge house with no heating. My toes were always blue. I believe in my heart that their frugality caused me my dad's Raynaud's. My mom would complain that I needed to just wear more layers. My father and I literally wore bootleg gloves inside the house. Sometimes they were leopard print and said "J.Dew" instead of "J.Crew."

But it was a blessing. Being cheap came in handy when I moved to NYC, the most expensive city in America. I cooked every single one of my meals and brought a Tupperware container of quinoa, vegetables, and canned sardines with me wherever I went. The only times I really ate out were when some dude was paying. (Which, as I mentioned earlier, rarely happened. They were as stingy with their money as they were with their boners.)

My mom's complete disregard for beauty allowed me to

ignore all of the bullshit in Hollywood. My mom never got facials or pedicures, and she's still better looking than me. I recently put a Bioré strip on her to rip out her blackheads. The white piece of paper looked like a hairbrush afterward. It was so deeply satisfying. My older sister came into my bathroom five minutes after I peeled it off my mom's face to ask me a question. I kicked her out and said, "Go back to the living room, I need at least ten more minutes to be alone with the strip." If you girls ever want to see the strip, just go to the living room and look above the television: I plan on framing it.

Even now, after some success, I'm so terribly cheap, but I think it's a good thing. I maintain a friendship with a woman that I hate simply because she has a lemon tree. I wear the same $19.99 digital Casio watch that I've had forever. I picked up your used infant whale bathtub from somebody's lawn in the neighborhood (I still don't know who this person is and if they made meth in that tub or what). I eat eggs that are two weeks past their expiration date. (I don't really believe that eggs expire. I mean do you know what an expired egg even looks like?) My pajamas are all regular clothes that have gone out of style (if you're lucky, you might be wearing some of my Ed Hardy jogging pajamas right now!). I keep a bag of hotel slippers and refuse to buy my own. But I paid off the mortgage on our home!

Another instrumental Asian value is bluntness. My parents always found a way of saying things that you weren't supposed to. It used to embarrass me, but like the cheapness, now I'm so grateful for it. When my mom and I took a trip to Vietnam together shortly after my father passed, she came to lunch with Hai and about six of our mutual friends. I hadn't seen a lot of these people in so long and almost cried because I was so happy to be reunited in this beautiful country where we had all first met. When my mom greeted my friend Vinh, after not seeing him for many years, she noticed that he had gained a lot of weight and said to him, "Wow, Vinh, you look so prosperous." We all knew that she meant, "You got real fat." But she said it with such a matter-of-fact, unapologetic attitude that it didn't even offend him. All of our friends heard her and laughed because there was something so familiar and affectionate about her honesty. It just was what it was. Neither she, nor my father, nor me or any of my siblings could ever help but speak to exactly what was on our minds, no matter how inappropriate. Again, this was something that used to really bug the shit out of me. It was really embarrassing when my mom told one of my friends, "I want to see your nose job" after she got a nose job. When I was in Vietnam, I traveled to Phú Quốc, an island known for making fish sauce. I returned to Saigon with a bottle for my aunt Nga hoping that she would be excited. When she tasted it, she looked up at me and said: "What can I say? It's just not good."

But now, I love that my family taught me how to be refreshingly rude and honest. It also toughened me up and prepared me for bombing and criticism, because I had been humorlessly roasted by my family my whole life. People always tell me that they think stand-up comedy is so hard. But it's nothing compared to being hoorided constantly by the people who love you most and know you best. My mom used to say, "The tangerine skin is thick so you must have sharp nails." People like to praise Asian Americans as the model minority for their strong work ethic and good behavior. My

Vietnamese mother did not give me either. But she made me cheap, tough, and salty, like a steak from Sizzler.

When the movie *Crazy Rich Asians* first premiered, a very talented Asian American actress in her late forties, who I'll call Rebecca, admitted to me that she refused to watch the film, and would probably never see it, simply because she was jealous that she wasn't in it. As she looked down at her shoes, she confessed, "I just feel so left out."

I told her, "It's not your fault. You were made to feel that way. The lack of opportunities for Asian Americans in Hollywood conditioned you to be insecure and envious."

"You don't feel that way?" she asked me.

"Well, you're from a different generation, where the success of another Asian person drives you crazy because you were made to believe that there was only one spot available."

"You have no idea what it was like. Until very recently, every role I auditioned for required an accent."

"God, that sucks."

"Do you think I'm a monster? You must think I'm a fucking child," she said.

"I think you are being honest, which I always appreciate, and I get why you feel that way. I don't think you're a child, I think you're a human being who came up in this business at a shitty time."

For her, that was the truthful but ugly answer to the question, "What's it like to be an Asian American in Hollywood?" *Don't miss the one spot every ten years.*

I'll never forget that conversation because it made me realize how timing and my upbringing played such a significant role in shaping how I see myself and how I view my people. I have an unusual amount of Asian pride. My dad filled our house with Chinese stone carvings, antique furniture, screens, lamps, plants, and rugs. My parents exposed me to all the Wong Kar Wai films at a very early age and every year we attended the San Francisco International Asian American Film Festival together. In that Chinatown alleyway youth center that my dad grew up in I developed my first crushes on Asian American boys. I looked up to Asian American teenage girls with their crimped black hair and perfectly plucked black eyebrows. I traded mixtapes with and learned pager code from people who were also raised to take their shoes off when entering a home and who didn't smell like Kraft Singles.

But Rebecca grew up in a city on the East Coast, where she was extremely isolated from people who looked like her. That made her instinctively competitive when, all of a sudden, she finally was surrounded by women that looked exactly like her only because they were waiting to audition for the role of the wet-haired ghost from *The Ring* or Angry Waitress with Fake-Ass Accent #2. The "specialness" she was used to feeling from looking different vanished instantly. I also grew up feeling special because I was Asian, but for the opposite reason. Not because I was different from the people around me, but because I was the same as them, which filled me with pride and allowed me to avoid the "crabs in a bucket" mentality. (Also, we were in Chinatown and on Clement Street a lot, so I learned directly from seeing a lot of crabs in buckets.)

———

The other question young people always ask me is: "What advice do you have for a person like me, an Asian American woman wanting to get into Hollywood?" Here it is: Let go of seeing yourself as nothing more than an Asian American woman. Ask yourself who you are outside of that. Challenge yourself to get out of the community. Don't just drink boba, do your laundry at home, take pictures of food, go outlet shopping, and talk exclusively to other Asian Americans. Even if you end up doing something totally unrelated to entertainment, I want you to take this advice, because I want you to become interesting, confident, and cultured women. Expose yourself to how other people in America live, how they think, and you will discover the universal struggles that connect us all, like how we all sleep in hotel rooms and pretend they're not covered in the cum of a thousand dead lonely men. If you hang out with the same people, you will only be able to make those people laugh. Go to Burning Man. Travel to different cities in America. Travel the world. See concerts. Go to plays. Eat Ethiopian food. Introduce yourself to everything there is. When in doubt, go out. Not just for material, but to experience new people, new social situations, and unfamiliar surroundings. I used to hate going out, especially going out late. When I was living in NYC, Donald Glover invited me to one of the famous *SNL* parties that start at two A.M. and end at six A.M. I declined because I've always loved staying at home, getting in bed early, and the comfort of sitting on my own toilet. And I have a fear of being left alone at a party or someone feeling obligated to babysit me. But I should have gone. I was twenty-seven at the time, and I could've tried to trap fucking Donald Glover.

But don't get me wrong—it's also important to make friends with other Asian American people in entertainment. My two very best friends in the industry are Sheng Wang and Kevin Camia. I brought Kevin out to open for me on my first big tour and am currently bringing Sheng on the second one. Not only are they ridiculously funny, but both of them are like brothers to me. I have a brother, but I always wanted a *twin* brother because of the hit TV show *Beverly Hills, 90210*. I thought it would be so cool to have a built-in male best friend. A guy my same age who'd look out for me without any sexual tension. Sheng Wang is my Brandon Walsh. If you're too young to understand that reference, then he's my Ashley Olsen or one of those Winklevoss Facebook twins that are not as fun to look at as Armie Hammer.

Sheng is godfather to you. He was one of the first people to visit me in the hospital when I had each of you. I sharted *very* loudly in my hospital diaper, and he didn't even say anything about it because he's a good friend. He helped build your cribs and the rocking chair that I breastfed both of you in. Nikki projectile shat onto Sheng once. He lifted his feet up and screamed, "Did she get me? Did she get me?" And you did, Nikki. You nailed him. But he didn't care. I think he kind of liked it, actually. But not in a creepy way. When the babysitter cancels, we always call Uncle Sheng. He regularly picks up Mari from preschool when we can't, and has a car seat in his car, just for you guys. That is a real friend. And a real cheap way to get childcare.

When I first moved to Los Angeles, the comedian Bobby Lee picked me up from my apartment located at Crenshaw and Pico. When I got in his car, he said, "In all the years I've lived in this city, I have never been this far south in Los Angeles." He drove me to a Korean restaurant called Soot Bull Jeep that smelled like charcoal and beef. The staff, which consisted of warm, fifty-something women, all said "Hi, Bobby!" in Korean when we entered. When we sat down, he told me, "I'm older than you so of course I'm going to pay for everything. So get whatever you want." In Korean, he ordered enough food to feed five people and asked me about how things were going. Afterward, he dropped me back off at my apartment and didn't try to kiss me or anything. I always remember that because he was light-years ahead of me and didn't have to do that. This brother- and sisterhood with other Asian American people in entertainment—how they treat me and take care of me and demand other people respect me—has given me my community that keeps me protected. So I'm saying you need both—your community *and* what lies outside it.

My last piece of advice would be to focus not on the result, but instead, the process and the journey. Again, Asian people love predictable outcomes. But to succeed in a creative profession, you really need to love it. And if you love it and are great at it, and passionate about constantly becoming better at it, you will find success no matter what.

If not, you can always be a professional hoarder like your uncle Andrew (he would be so proud!!!).

CHAPTER 13

Bridin' Dirty

Dear Girls,

At weddings, I cry whenever a bride walks down the aisle, even if I don't know her that well. I cry for her because I can tell it's the first time she's had that many people look at her and watch her all at once. A wedding is an excuse to finally get a glam squad and peacock-feather the shit out of your inner goddess. It's an opportunity to make everyone stand up for you. It's a powerful feeling for the bride, and she's experiencing it for the first and potentially last time. I cry not because she looks beautiful, but because she looks dramatically different. And she put so much effort into looking transformed, and I feel like it would be a disservice to her if I didn't cry or yell out, "YOU LOOK GOOD, GURRRRRL!" Plus the expression on a bride's face is always the same—a little embarrassed, a little shy, and truly happy that everyone is there with her. But it's proud too. She knows she looks great.

She knows she looks her best. Because she put a lot of planning, money, and people in misery to design it this way. Plus she's excited to eat carbs and drink flavored beverages again.

But for me, it would've been my worst nightmare. Because of comedy, I've never had the desire to walk down an aisle slowly while three hundred people stare at me for two minutes, and not say anything. Usually when people all have their eyes on me in silence, that's a bad sign. I am not used to performing without talking, or performing for free. And I was in no mood to entertain those nearest and dearest to me on my wedding day.

I was twenty-eight when your father proposed and by then all of my very best friends had gotten married. At the time, I was living in NYC, acting on an ABC medical drama where I played a quirky agoraphobic radiologist who was in love with the hospital's plumber. I had to memorize dialogue like "If you use the tDCS I built you, the occipital lobe should demonstrate imaging of the new aneurysm, and we'll be using transcranial magnetic stimulation, magnetic coils to stimulate your medial prefrontal cortex, which regulates the amygdala, where fear memories are processed." When I wasn't trying to cram all of this insane craniotomy language into my head while riding the subway, I was doing nine stand-up sets a night because I did not want to say these complicated-ass words I didn't understand on camera for the rest of my life. The added task of planning a wedding was highly unappealing. I watched friends torture themselves (and me) over centerpieces and felt like I'd rather spend my nights doing those stand-up sets than pinteresting invitation fonts. There's enough event planning I have to do in my professional life, and I wanted to make the wedding as simple as possible. So I went on the SF.GOV website and paid the fifteen-dollar registration fee to get married at city hall. It was very important that it was in San Francisco, where all of the Wongs live. None of my family had to get on an airplane. We didn't have to pay for any decor because we already paid for the city hall decor with our *tax dollars*. It's hard to beat the combination of consideration and value in one event.

Before the ceremony, we waited in line behind three other couples who were like us: too cheap and lazy to have a real wedding. In a room that looked like that underground bunker they found in *Lost*, we signed some documents that I did not fully read, registering us as a married couple. I still don't know or remember if I checked a box agreeing to donate all of my organs to any government official of San Francisco if I was ever found mildly unconscious.

For the actual ceremony, we just invited our immediate family and one best friend each. My three nephews wore ties and my niece wore an eighty-dollar Tiffany-blue dress and blush. She was so excited, she arrived with her own bouquet. An elderly woman with a nose piercing and black graduation cloak officiated the five-minute-long ceremony. While all of my friends had met with the pastors or rabbis who married them multiple times before the big day, I had never seen this lady before in my life and forgot her name immediately after she introduced herself. At the end of the ceremony, which ended with "by the power of the state of California, I now pronounce you married," I said, "Hey, can we say some vows?" She looked at me as if I asked, "Hey, can we sleep in city hall overnight and have you cuddle with us?" and firmly responded, "No." My father-in-law, your grandpa, made his fortune by selling Wacky Wallwalkers—those little sticky octopuses that would come in your cereal in the 1980s. You'd throw them against the wall and they would eventually crawl down to the floor. They're very symbolic and sacred objects to him, so naturally, he tossed a bunch of them at us at the end, in place of the traditional rice. Judge Moody made us clean it all up off the floor immediately afterward and rushed us out of the beautiful mid-century modern rotunda.

That evening, we all went out to eat at my favorite Chinese restaurant in San Francisco, R & G Lounge. In a small private room with two large tables, we feasted on a ten-course meal while everyone, except for the kids, gave speeches. It was nice to be able to just sit back, enjoy the speeches, and listen to everyone else talk about us. So, having found a work-around that actually worked, here is some advice on how to do a wedding right:

1. **Get a Chinese banquet.** A lot of Asian American kids are averse to the Chinese banquet because it does not provide the most idyllic ambiance. The waitstaff are dressed in maroon bow ties with matching maroon vests and the tablecloths are always pink. Most of my peers would rather get married in a rustic barn and put a bunch of tea lights in mason jars and cover everything in muslin and rosemary. The couple is eating by themselves at a distressed white desk for no reason. To me, a wedding is not an excuse to Instagram or drink Moscow Mules. Chinese people believe a wedding should be a profitable venture to favorably position the newly married couple for the journey ahead. A Western wedding that serves Western food typically costs at least a hundred dollars per person. Yes, the Western model is a buffet of photo opportunities, but leads to heavy spending and debt that could otherwise be spent on a house, one day of preschool, or a cool

Japanese toilet that cleans itself. (Hopefully by the time you're adults, all toilets will be Toto toilets. Hopefully writing that sentence will get our family a free Toto toilet.) Our banquet cost thirty dollars per person. Vietnamese people do the Chinese banquet even though they're Vietnamese because they cannot resist the great deal. Our menu consisted of ten delicious and mysterious courses (such as sautéed geoduck clam with bamboo pith rolls and sea cucumber) and everyone left very full, and with a ton of leftovers. My niece, who was six years old at the time, giggled as her mother tucked a napkin into the neck of her satin dress, in anticipation of the salt and pepper crab arriving to her on the lazy Susan. She and my three nephews all screamed in delight as my mom showed them how to crack the shells by themselves for the first time. My best friend, Miya, was just silent for five minutes straight, focused on digging for any remnants of flesh inside the claw with her chopstick. Crab juice, crab meat, and crab shells were flying around the table, staining everyone's suits and dresses, including mine, and nobody gave a fuck, because nothing was expensive. We were slurping, cracking, chewing, and laughing with the people we loved most.

2. **Never have a destination wedding.** The first one I ever went to required that we stay in cabins. I had to bring *provisions*. I packed things one should never have to pack for a wedding, like a compass and some iodine tablets. I was forced to spend Memorial Day weekend with a bunch of random alcoholics in their late forties because my friend in her late twenties mar-

ried someone in his late forties. (Don't do this please.
It's almost as bad as me catching you eating at a P. F.
Chang's.) I do not like how destination weddings rob
you of your vacation weekends, which were everything
to me when I was working as a receptionist. The worst
was a wedding we went to in the Catskills. We had to
take a train from NYC into the forest, and then rent a
car just to get even deeper into the forest. The food
was kosher and happened to have no flavor. There was
one grocery store within thirty miles that served sandwiches. I have never eaten so many Italian subs in one
weekend. I pounded subs, went to the reception, and
then got my period at this cabin on top of a mountain,
like some salami goddess of fertility. I needed a tam-
pon, but that grocery store at the bottom of the
mountain was closed by then, so I had to stuff my
underwear with toilet paper like a savage, like a teenage girl ashamed of getting her period, too shy to ask
for a pad. My least favorite song, the Black Eyed Peas
frat boy anthem "I Gotta Feeling," started playing
while I was leaking all over my skirt and starving because the kosher dinner was awful. Nobody noticed
me sobbing because all the guests were busy screaming "Tonight's gonna be a good niiiiiiiight!" I hate
that song because (a) it sucks and (b) it somehow plays
every time I'm having a bad night.

3. **Buy your dress on eBay.** I tried on a BCBG dress
in store that was way out of my price range before
your father even proposed. So when I finally got engaged, I already had put it in my cart on eBay, where
I found it used for a third of the price. And you best

believe I bought it the very damn day I got engaged. It was $250 and by far the most I had ever spent on a dress at that point. I stepped on it right when we were walking up the steps into city hall. My heel ripped this big hole on the bottom. And instead of crying, I laughed. It was good luck, and I didn't care because I hadn't blown a fortune on it. It was just for that day. And now it's sitting in a box in the garage. So it's there, if you guys ever want to play dress up in it, or, if you're desperate for cash, resell it on eBay to some creepy male fan of mine so that he can put it on his hairy body and do impressions of me in front of a full-length mirror in his parents' basement while whispering "I'd fuck me" over and over.

4. **Get your hair done at a blowout bar.** It's $40 versus $500 for someone to come over to your house and do it. Do the math.

5. **Don't have a wedding party.** I didn't have any bridesmaids because, in the past, I had rejected so many of my friends' requests to be theirs. Every time someone asked me to be a bridesmaid, I felt like they were asking "Hey, do you want to be financially burdened?" I caved in a total of two times. The first time I did it, I hardly participated. I didn't even go to the bachelorette party. It made no sense to spend an entire weekend in Cabo San Lucas with a bunch of women I'd never met before. Again, I hate it when people rob me of my vacation weekends. I'm not trying to spend Memorial Day with a friend's co-worker named Bethany who wears fake eyelashes every day and just downloaded a meditation app. Some brides are not a

trustworthy hub for female friends. Some brides surround themselves with superficial twats or disturbing dweebs. There's always some weirdo cousin with no social skills and a shady frenemy from the past who used to steal makeup, boyfriends, and clothes from the bride. And then I don't understand why we're celebrating with all of these dicks. And why are we wearing them around our necks? Unless we're a tribe of kick-ass Amazonians and those penises are war trophies, I don't want to wear them. I want a *real* dick before I get married. Not a sweet-and-sour-candy pretend-dick strung around my neck. One bride kept pressuring me to host and said, "You're the best person to do it." And I was like, "Oh, I KNOW I'm the best person to do it. I'm not going to do it."

The second time I was a bridesmaid was for my best friend, Miya. I was genuinely happy to do it since all of her friends were warm, smart, and fun. I delegated the shit out of them. I put myself in charge of dinner but the limo reservation, spa destination, and everything else was in the hands of these other responsible-ass women. It was a great experience overall but the speech was a stressful homework assignment. I felt a lot of pressure to be funny and moving and sweet. The stakes were very high because it wasn't for money, it was for my *best friend* and the audience was not anonymous. If I ate it in front of her mom and her husband's cute cousin who I plan to marry in the next lifetime, and *then* had to attend the rest of the wedding soaked in the shame of a bomb instead of leaving the theater like usual, I would have changed my name and moved to Vancouver.

6. Have your bachelorette party at Disneyland.
After I had my miscarriage, my best friend came to L.A. I wanted to feel like my old self and be able to make light of the situation so we got extremely high. We each ate half of a chocolate cannabis heart. Later, a co-worker told me I should have eaten an eighth of the heart. Everyone in Los Angeles has some sort of Disneyland hookup. One of our friends had a brother who was a dancer. Another woman's sister-in-law was a storyboarder for Disney. So we all went for free. Soaring over California was magical, because I was so high. And It's a Small World made me feel like the world really *was* small, after all (I was high as shit). Space Mountain made me feel like I was in space (I don't think I've even been that high). But then Indiana Jones was awful. That big ball threatening to crush me and that huge snake hissing in my face felt like I was about to die in the worst way possible. Do not get high and then go on Indiana Jones. Consider this your one and only warning. Anyway, then we went to a Napa restaurant, where they laid out all of these candy penises. The key to this whole thing is being high. Going to Disneyland sober for a bachelorette party would be an absolute waste of time.

7. Keep it super small. We just invited our families and our number one best friend. Nobody could feel left out because *nobody* was invited, and we got to spend quality time with our guests.

8. Make it all about the speeches. As I said, at the Chinese banquet following our wedding, it was so small that every single person gave a toast. It was personal and entertaining and *free*. It's the best way to inject quality into the experience without paying top dollar for an Asian Adele impersonator you saw on YouTube.

9. **Chill out.** A wedding is not a marriage. It's one day of celebration, one of hopefully many with the love of your life. I'm so proud of how your father and I began our marriage by carving our own path in life and didn't get sucked into the mainstream take on "how things are done" despite feeling a lot of pressure to spend a ton of money on it all. We knew the journey ahead was going to be filled with expensive-ass purchases like a house and childcare for you little unborn ladies.

I have zero regrets about how your father and I got married. Now I'm at the age where people are getting divorced, and they wish they hadn't spent so much on their weddings. When my sister Julia got married, she spent a lot of time and effort putting together a beautiful wedding at a museum for over a hundred attendees. I had never met half of them in my life. There was a chocolate fondue fountain. Julia took a ton of time planning the food, the invitations, and the decor. She also asked my other sister, Mimi, to please shave her armpits and legs, which Mimi hadn't done in twenty years and hasn't done since. Everything had been meticulously orchestrated, and she didn't ask anyone in our family to make a speech except for me. Before the first course came out, my dad clinked on a glass with a fork, and unexpectedly sang a personalized song about my sister and her husband to the tune of "America the Beautiful." Everyone was laughing until my mom went up to ask him to stop, and he exclaimed, "Tammy, get away from me!" which, while it would make a great country song, is not a great thing to yell at your wife at your daughter's wedding. Right then, everyone saw a glimpse of their not-so-perfect marriage, and looked down at their laps uncomfortably while my dad continued with two more verses of his song as though it was still fun and funny.

My sister, understandably, was very upset. Our dad had coerced her three-man string band into playing the instrumentals, he had fucked up the timing of dinner, and he straight up embarrassed her. My dad was a well-intentioned and fun-loving guy, and it all would've been fine if it was just our family because we're all comfortable with the fact that our family is weird as shit. But he loved the spotlight and the captive audience. The whole thing caused a lot of tension and a lot of charged emotions, which is very dicey and stressful to have at the start of a marriage. There is enough going on, no need to add wedding drama to the mix, especially in front of all those damn people.

If you happen to get married at city hall in SF, and the judge with the nose ring is still alive, ask her if you can read vows and when she says no, tell her she let your mom do it.

CHAPTER 14

Wild Child

Dear Girls,

I have another confession to make: I was an awful teenager and that resulted in a very tense relationship with my mother, and if karma is real (it is), then all of my bad behavior will come back to haunt me (oh God).

When I was a junior in high school, I went to a pajama-themed party where I started randomly dancing with a senior from another, much cooler high school. Students there tended to be more focused on arts and unconventional learning. He wore a big, puffy, black North Face vest over a flannel shirt with cargo pants, which was *not* in line with the theme, but it was the dress code to my heart. His outfit was simultaneously tough and laid back and, most important, warm. We barely spoke as he lifted up my leg and we dry humped (I mean danced!) in front of everyone to Tupac's "California Love" while taking turns chugging on the same forty-ounce bottle of Mickey's malt liquor. Later that night, we ended up on my parents' living room couch, between antique Chinese lamps and stone carvings, doing everything but the nasty. I didn't hear from him at all afterward and wasn't even sure he knew my name. If he hadn't gone to a school where we had mutual friends, I definitely wouldn't have remembered his. Months later, he called for the first time to invite me to his prom, and I spontaneously asked him to mine as well. I had a great time at his prom and liked him so much that I was very nervous about hosting him at mine. I had hopes that he could be my San Francisco version of a quarterback boyfriend. Instead of impressing people by knowing all the game-winning plays, he would impress them by knowing all the members of The Hieroglyphics! My school's prom itself was kind of boring for him, because the kids were a lot more academic, stiff, and not as into dancing, and none of his friends were there. I caught him peeking at his watch several times throughout the night. Then at an afterparty in Marin, I thought I'd loosen him up if I myself loosened up, by guzzling malt liquor and vodka. This led to me throwing up in the host's bed and then getting punched in the face by his equally drunk friend, who, I guess, was very protective of his homie's mattress. The guy with the North Face vest escaped to another party that night and never called me again.

Here are just a few examples of other shameful things I did in my youth, off the top of my head:

- I smoked my first cigarette when I was eleven years old.
- I regularly shoplifted Wet n Wild lipstick, electric-blue eyeshadow, and Wet Seal flared jeans. (The word "wet" made products one hundred percent

more appealing to me as a teen, which is odd in retrospect, because when you're a teen, that's the time when you need the least help as a woman in getting wet.)

- I wore scarf wrap shirts, with no bra, exposing my entire back, from this store called Bebe—an outfit that made the Kardashians look like background actors in *The Handmaid's Tale*.

- I bought my first marijuana pipe at age fourteen.

- I dated a man who had *graduated* from college when I was still in high school.

- I dated men who never went to college or graduated from high school when they were at the age where they should've graduated from college . . . when I was still in high school.

- As soon as I got my driver's license, I attempted a three-point turn on a very narrow block and accidentally hit two parked vehicles with my mom's gold Volvo station wagon.

- I tried taking laxatives for a week to make myself lose weight.

- I once dropped an empty forty-ounce bottle of Olde English malt liquor from a twenty-story building onto the street and could've killed any pedestrian walking underneath.

- I constantly hoped my mother would get sent to the mom version of Alcatraz.

- I pretended to be sick in bed on very challenging test days.

- One New Year's Eve when I was seventeen, I made out with thirteen boys and three girls. That's basically an entire high school production of *Oliver!*

There are many more appalling things I did that I'm way too ashamed to include in this list. To this day, I still feel consequences from my bad behavior. During my senior year of high school, I constantly wore four-inch platforms from Aldo because I was very insecure about my prepubescent body, and was convinced those ridiculous sandals would increase my sex appeal. I can tell you now that nobody wants to fuck you more because you're four inches higher off the ground due to shoes that smell like Eternity For Men and cost $39.99 with the second pair half off. At one party where I was wearing my signature space shoes, I started jumping with my friend on her bed like it was a trampoline and I sprained my ankle. The next day my entire left foot looked like I had been stepping in a bucket of blueberries. It was so badly bruised that one podiatrist asked if he could submit the X-ray to a medical journal that I assumed was called *Terrible Feet Monthly*. I re-injure it every three to five years. It still gives me pain at night and is one of the main reasons I am grateful that marijuana is legal in California.

In sixth grade, at the day camp I attended, I had a huge crush on this boy named Jake King. He was half white, half Laotian, very tall, ate ketchup with spaghetti—all of which I found very endearing at the time (that dish is now a sign that somebody is a serial killer). I liked him so much that I decided to do something awful to him so he'd like me back. I figured out that if you pressed hard on the red highlighted word "occupied" on a porta potty and just slid it clockwise to "vacant," it would unlock the bathroom. I opened the door on Jake while he was taking a shit. About ten other kids who were waiting in line laughed hysterically—some of them had to sit down on the woodchips because they were laughing so hard—as Jake sat frozen on the toilet seat, with his pants down at his ankles. Eventually he put his head in his hands, and I knew right away that I had failed as a pickup artist. I closed the door, feeling really bad about embarrassing him. I had crossed the line from a playful neg to the summer camp equivalent of Cersei's walk of shame. I volunteered at the same camp in my twenties, when he was a leader as well, and the first thing he said to me was: "Hey, remember when you opened the door while I was taking a shit and everyone laughed at me?" And I did. Because you never forget something like that.

———

Even now, I'm not sure if I was actually wild or if I just wanted to *seem* like I was wild. I attended private schools with mostly white people, and while I didn't have problems making friends, I never felt like my peers were my tribe. I never felt fully comfortable or at home with my classmates, so being regarded as a little crazy was my way of fitting in and getting friends.

Since my siblings were all so much older, I desperately wanted to grow up and be part of their world as soon as possible. *Part of their world.* I'm just realizing right now that that is probably why I love *The Little Mermaid* so much. I could not wait to catch up to my beautiful older sisters. In elementary school, I shoved their retired retainers in my mouth because I just wanted to feel what it was like to be old enough to need orthodontic care. My music taste was about ten years ahead of all my peers. I'm pretty sure I was the only third-grader who listened to Annie Lennox, 10,000 Maniacs, and De La Soul. I read *Backlash* by Susan Faludi when I was in fifth grade and didn't understand any of it but I wanted to identify with *feminist rage*! In elementary school, I would also romanticize having my period, and sometimes wore my sister's thick-ass maxi pads recreationally, under my yellow Esprit leggings. From the outside my vagina looked like a giant plantain that could yield a heaping plate of tostones. I am certain that part of my bad behavior was a concerted effort to grow up faster than my parents or biology would allow.

I shoplifted because it was thrilling to get something for free, to not have to ask permission from my parents to get makeup. I had worn uniforms forever, and they were oversized uniforms, no less. My mom bought them used. And they never fit me. The skirt always hung down to my ankles. I looked like the little boy Tom Hanks turns back into at the end of *Big*. My mom was scared of me growing out of my clothes and just wanted to buy one uniform. So high school was extra exciting because I got to dress myself. That's why I exposed my body with those ridiculous outfits—because feeling sexy and, hopefully, desired was a new frontier, especially coming from an all-girls school. I dated an older man because the Asian American classmates my age didn't make me feel older, so I had to outsource one that made me feel sexy beyond my years. No big psychological underpinning to when I dropped that forty-ounce bottle from that high-rise, though. I just did that because I was drunk from downing that forty.

Now I'm thinking more about *The Little Mermaid*, and I think that movie is the reason I flirted with anorexia as well. As you know, it was my absolute favorite movie growing up, and deep down I always wanted to have a tiny waist and big boobies and a collection of broken forks like Ariel. Now, as the mother of you two girls, I see that whole story line as my worst nightmare. It's a terrible fable about a girl who leaves her family and sacrifices her voice for a boy that she's never even met. *Bitch, WHAT are you doing?? Get back in the fucking water!* We are never watching that movie again after the next time we watch it.

Honestly, my entire high school was anorexic. All the girls drank Diet Coke and, when offered ice cream or cake, looked like they'd just discovered a turd in their backpack. For your average teenager, I considered myself to have a high level of self-esteem but, even so, I couldn't escape body image issues. I'm gonna show you pictures of me during that summer in Hawai'i, when I was more than twenty pounds heavier, and looked like a coconut with glasses, but had the best time of my life. Nobody else gets to see those!

My mom kept generalizing my bad behavior as my "teen-age phase," which of course incensed me even more. We fought so much that when I'd try to really communicate with her about how I felt, she'd cover her ears, walk away from me, and scream, "YOU'RE GIVING ME A HEADACHE!" I thought my mom was the coldest, cruelest, and most annoy-ing person in the world. As I said, until very recently, I had a lot of resentment toward her.

I used to think we didn't get along because of cultural dif-ferences. Because she grew up in Vietnam, her school days were frequently interrupted by bombings, and she had to run in her áo dài uniform into a shelter. Meanwhile, I ditched class to drink malt liquor in a playground. We grew up in dif-ferent countries with different recreational activities and con-flicting concepts of what is acceptable for a young woman to do. It blew her mind that my siblings and I had friends of the opposite sex. Men were people who paid for meals because they wanted to eventually procreate with you. Other than that, why on earth would you have fun talking to them? What could you possibly have in common if they had a dick? It's really rare for any immigrant mother to see any value in hav-ing a platonic male friend.

My dad was the first and ONLY person my mother ever even *kissed*. In Vietnam, during those days especially, kissing someone basically meant you were going to get married. So my mom could never coach me on how to handle heartbreak, because she had never experienced it.

I was always so jealous of my white friends who got pedicures with their mothers. I didn't get my first one until I was twenty-seven. The poor woman who resembled all of my aunties looked at my feet and let out an audible sigh which roughly translated to: "Are you kidding with this shit?" It was a big task at hand. She carved out my toenails that were buried in twenty-seven years of cuticle skin. As she hacked away, it looked like it was snowing from my feet. And I couldn't believe it only cost twenty dollars to have her do that.

I know it seems like mani-pedis are laced into Vietnamese women's DNA. Vietnamese American people *are* really good at doing black and white women's nails. But it's not really part of Vietnamese culture to get our *own* nails done. Getting your nails done was seen as not only a huge waste of money and time, but a huge nuisance when you were preparing food with your bare hands (nobody wears gloves in Vietnam, except to shield their hands from the sun or commit murders). I love my mom and I will never be as beautiful as her, but her feet definitely do not match her face. Her toenails are so thick and dark, they look like little barnacles on the bottom of a ship. Whenever I try to convince her to get a pedicure, she grabs her heels and screams, "No, I need my calluses!" That's how third world my mom is. She's grateful for her hard layers of skin and wants to keep them, just in case there's some kind of mass shoe extinction.

In college, the debauchery continued but at least my mom and dad didn't have to smell my malt liquor breath and deal with my fractured body parts firsthand. At UCLA, I peed in public parking lots and on public streets, at night, without toilet paper, conservatively, three hundred times. I would wipe my vagina with a friend's unused menstrual pad or one of my socks and then throw it into the bushes. I ran with a pack of Asian American women and men that were like me, extremely academic and equally wild. One of the guys, Quoc, was born the day after me and we always had a party at someone's apartment to celebrate our birthdays together. At my twentieth birthday, there happened to be plenty of vodka but no chaser like orange juice or soda. There was only a gallon of milk in the fridge. After a couple of shots I decided to wash down the vodka with milk even though I was lactose intolerant. I spent the second half of my twentieth birthday just farting, body rolling to Ludacris's "Southern Hospitality," and barfing, and then more farts.

UCLA offered students the opportunity to watch the latest movies for two dollars on campus and I always made sure to see them when I could. After I watched *Hedwig and the Angry Inch*, I went on to see it in the theater ten more times. I was so moved by the character Hedwig, who just wanted to be loved and was stuck performing in these shitty venues in front of six people (foreshadowing my time on the open mic circuit). She was damaged and talented and abandoned. I loved how Hedwig committed one hundred percent and gave her all to these shows, despite their obvious lack of mainstream appeal. During my sophomore year, John Cameron Mitchell, one of the co-creators and the original Hedwig, was judging a costume contest in West Hollywood. My college roommate Vanessa and I knew we couldn't compete with all of the men in drag dressed as Hedwig.

First, we decided that we had to go naked to even get noticed. And then we quickly realized you can't just win a costume contest by showing up naked. So that was out.

Then we had another idea. One of my favorite parts of *Hedwig and the Angry Inch* is the animation sequence that accompanies "The Origin of Love," a song based on a story from Plato's *Symposium,* about how we were all once two beings in one, and then got split up by jealous Greek gods. The song concludes that making love is when you find your other half. Vanessa and I decided to paint our bodies with iconic symbols and images from the song. We dumped $180 worth of latex body paint on our bedroom floor, which our other friend, Crystal, a very talented artist, used as her palette. With her hands, Crystal brushed blue and white strokes all over my body to symbolize water while Vanessa embodied fire. While she painted a huge yellow lightning bolt over my breasts, she casually said, "At first your boob is a boob. It's like, wow, I'm touching another woman's boob. And then after painting it awhile, it's just a boob." Crystal went on to paint a whale on my back, the earth on one of Vanessa's boobs, and then an eye on the other.

After the sing-along movie screening, Vanessa and I went up onstage with all of these men who looked even better than the original Hedwig. The best one had Hedwig's signature Farrah Fawcett blond wig, electric-blue eyeshadow, red lips, and denim romper with the grand cape reading in graffiti YANKEE GO HOME WITH ME. But thanks to Crystal, we managed to win the fucking contest and I kissed John Cameron Mitchell on the lips. I was in public naked with my nipples out, and even though I believe in #FreeTheNipple in principle, now, as a mother, I would still prefer MY daughters not free their nipples. Please focus on freeing dolphins and political prisoners instead.

I raged during the summers as well. Between my junior and senior years of college, I served food in the dining halls at Lair of the Golden Bear, a family camp for UC Berkeley alumni. I had grown up going to this camp for one week every summer, because my dad graduated from UC Berkeley. While I staffed there, they posted a weekly list of who had "groveled," meaning who had hooked up, in order to keep any romance known to all and discourage people from getting too possessive and jealous in what was meant to be a summer of fun. I made an appearance on that list with eight different people. I wish making that list had been my job, instead of serving tomato soup and grilled cheese sandwiches from a cart.

The problem was that, because my whole identity was wrapped up in being "wild," I couldn't turn it off, even after college. In my late twenties, I hooked up with a yoga instructor that I met at a bar. He looked like a young, punk-rock Clint Eastwood with jet-black hair. I know that sounds frightening but google-image "young Clint Eastwood" and I promise it will make you forget all about that whole empty chair speech he made as an old man. We had drinks on our first outing. When we went back to his friend's place where he was staying and started kissing, I immediately pulled away and warned him, "Hey, I'm on my period." He stood up, pulled down his pants, and said, "Well, then let's make a fucking mess, Ali." He didn't care about his penis looking like a weapon used in a murder. But I was too scared because *we had just met*. On our second outing he made me a vegan dinner (that's where I stole that move!) and we definitely took it all the way that night. At the time, he was just visiting SF, and was living on the side of a mountain in his aunt's cabin. After he left, I missed him, his cooking, and his penis so much that I flew to the Midwest in the middle of winter to visit him. At night he made me crabs, and in the morning he made me pancakes and bacon. We did yoga and had lots and lots of sex. On the second day at the cabin, I said, "Boy it's pretty nutty I came all the way out here after just meeting you. You're not crazy, right?"

He smiled and shook his head.

And then I laughed and said, "Great, well, I guess it's too late anyway. If you're gonna kill me nobody will be able to stop you."

Then, when I moved to New York to pursue stand-up, he came to pick me up and help carry my two huge suitcases up the four flights of stairs, to my very first New York apartment: a crusty Bed-Stuy shithole. He'd visit me intermittently, giving me a great sense of comfort and home in a very lonely time. When I moved again in the city, his childhood friend worked at a diner around the corner and we talked about how hard it was living in NYC. We had pleasant small conversations about her dear friend and she'd always offer me a free slice of apple pie.

One day she yelled to me in panic as I was walking past the diner. "Ali! Have you seen our friend?! You don't know this but he has multiple personality disorder and he's gone missing!"

I replied, "Oh my God . . . Can . . . Do I still get free pie?"

I tried to help her out but the only thing going through my head was, *Well, good thing I'm alive!* He could've so easily cut me up into a million pieces and used me as fertilizer for the cabin's garden. I wouldn't have even blamed him—that's how stupid meeting someone you don't know on a mountain is.

———

I fantasized about having a mother who was also raised on *Sesame Street,* Happy Meals, and John Hughes movies. Maybe she could ask me white mom questions like "How are you feeling?" or say white mom things like "I love you to the moon and back." We would share the same first language. She could help me pick out a dress that I actually liked, instead of the dress that was most discounted. We would *understand* each other and not fight as much.

But I recently saw that hipster movie *Lady Bird* and realized white chicks have issues with their mothers too. Yes, it took me that long to realize it.

So all I can do right now is hope that our relationship, especially when you two are teenagers, will be better than mine was with my mom. We get along great now that I have kids, but those early years were really painful. As long as you don't get maimed or contract life-threatening STDs, I accept that some shit is going to go down.

Please know you can talk to me more than I was able to talk to my mother. We have the same first language. We will have read the same books, like *Corduroy* and *Charlotte's Web,* and have a much more shared experience of growing up. It's already so wonderful that Mari demands to watch Hayao Miyazaki movies every time we get into the minivan because I love *Ponyo* and *My Neighbor Totoro* too. I hope you also like the Harry Potter books and hiking and s'mores and *Sixteen Candles* (even though the Long Duk character is an abomination). I want to be a confidant for you little ladies. I'll give you makeup tips if you want them (really, I just have one:

Never use a black eyebrow pencil or you'll look like you have caterpillars crawling above your eyes).

For International Day at my school, I decided in sixth grade to dress up in my mom's old áo dài, that traditional Vietnamese silk dress that has a collar, long sleeves, and is worn with pants. Well, in sixth grade, I couldn't even fit my arm into a dress my mom wore when she was eighteen years old. She loved bragging to her friends and family afterward about how she was so skinny in her youth that even her twelve-year-old prepubescent daughter couldn't squeeze into her past silhouette. I've saved a box of my dresses, in hopes that you girls will take an interest in them one day, and because since we all grew up eating cheese and croissants from Costco, you'll probably fit into them. I promise things get way better after your teenage years. I look forward to us being adults together. I can't think that far ahead, and I know things never turn out how you think they will, but I'm hopeful.

by Justin Hakuta

Dear Mari and Nikki,

Your grandfather once told me that when I find the right opportunity in life, all of my prior random experiences will suddenly fit together and make sense. This is what happened when I met your mother.

My path to the illustrious Alexandra Dawn Wong began early, in Washington, D.C., in the 1980s. I was the middle of three boys, Uncle Kenzo was the oldest and Uncle Akira the youngest. We grew up on a steady diet of Japanese BB guns, *The Far Side* comics, *Fist of the North Star* anime, and Street Fighter II on Super Nintendo. Uncle Kenzo brought home albums like Nas's *Illmatic* and A Tribe Called Quest's *Low End Theory*. We lived in Cleveland Park in an Art Deco home, separated from the political world that surrounded us. Everything about my childhood primed me as a match for your mother.

Thanks to your brilliant lola, we were also fed a steady diet of traditional food from Capiz, Philippines, home of the folkloric vampire-like spirit known as "aswang." We emerged from music, video games, film, and the mix of Japanese and African American culture we consumed in our rooms to dine on her version of Filipino adobo. I watched her cook juicy chicken thighs, chicken drumsticks, small pork ribs, and tender chunks of beef perfectly marinated in soy sauce and vinegar until they transformed into deep brown deliciousness. Your mother had a similar childhood experience savoring the tapioca soup and pork your grandma Wong cooked for her in San Francisco. Even our palates were primed for connection.

On weekends your grandparents took me and your uncles to eat and grocery shop at Lotte Plaza Market in Virginia, a Korean grocery store where my staple was a piping hot bowl of beef udon. Your great-grandfather Hajime was a big believer in traditional Chinese medicine, and in turn your grandfather sourced medicines like bitter reishi tea and powdered deer antler to help alleviate my asthma and eczema. This a prelude to your mother and my openness to holistic medicine.

Heavily influenced by Uncle Kenzo's affinity for hip-hop, which led him into graffiti, DJing, and mixtapes, in high school I immersed myself in the local rap scene and I freestyled in ciphers filled with beatboxers, emcees, and singers, ever the odd Asian in the group. Thanks to my extensive music collection, a CD burner, AOL hip-hop chat rooms, and your grandfather's office mailroom, in the nineties I built a thriving rogue online business selling bootleg custom hip-hop CDs that enabled me to forgo summer jobs (until I realized it was illegal and stopped). I was imbibing a diverse mix of pop culture and traditional Asian sources that would later enable me to connect deeply with your mother: my love for Wu-Tang Clan matched by her love for Souls of Mischief.

Like both of you, I grew up in a household with a celebrity: my dad, your grandpa Ken. In the eighties and early nineties, he was known publicly as Dr. Fad. Grandpa Ken grew up in Kamakura, Japan, home of beautiful Buddhist temples and murasaki imo (delicious, purple sweet potato) soft-serve ice cream. As your mother wrote, in the eighties he brought the Wacky Wallwalker, a sticky rubber octopus toy, over from Japan and sold more than two hundred million of them. Everyone I knew had one of these toys. He was a very successful businessman, and was also the host of the popular kids' invention show, *The Dr. Fad Show*. The show was so popular in the nineties that Grandpa Ken was asked—donning a white sweatshirt with colorful Wacky Wallwalkers stitched all over it—to be a guest on *Late Night with Conan O'Brien* and *The Tonight Show* with Jay Leno. He even had a cartoon Christmas special about Wacky Wallwalkers called *Deck the Halls with Wacky Walls* that aired on NBC in 1983.

I didn't realize it back then, but, similar to your mother, Grandpa Ken was one of the few Asian American faces on television at the time. Later in life, I would come to realize how empowering it was to have a father who lived his passions and didn't let the fact that he was the only Asian person in the room hold him back. Watching your grandpa Ken defy racial and career norms to build his own creative universe ranging from toys to television and art, your uncles and I directly experienced how full the world is of creative opportunity. There was no bamboo ceiling for us. We were free to carve our own paths as individuals, a drive and passion I later recognized in your mother when we first met.

I remember walking down the street as a family when I

was around eight years old and two white teenagers started saying "ching, chang, chong" as they passed us. I remember being called "chink" in a football game in high school and the next kickoff sprinting toward that person and drilling them into the ground. Racism and stereotypes are unavoidable and not everyone will understand where you come from, but having Grandpa Ken, similar to your mother today, embrace being an Asian entertainer on TV with such fearlessness, a pioneer on the airwaves, taught me pride and showed me that representation matters. This is why I buy you Asian Barbie dolls and children's books with faces that look like yours: because I want you to grow up immersed in role models that look familiar, so that you too can be inspired and live in a world of creative possibilities. By the time I met your mother, I was able to draw from my childhood experience with Grandpa Ken to recognize and support the unique path your mother was forging for herself.

I remember when I was about six years old I was playing by myself next to the living room with a mix of G. I. Joes, Thundercats action figures, and oxtail bones from a delicious soup your lola made that I had eaten clean, washed, and then used as spaceships. Grandpa Ken was walking by and saw me playing. He stopped and watched me for a bit, then asked me if I wanted him to draw something for me. I eagerly nodded yes, and he grabbed a blue marker and proceeded to draw a simple but effective fighter jet. I loved the drawing, but even more so I loved that I had his undivided attention for those few precious moments. There are, of course, challenges to having a famous parent. To be famous is to be in demand. As children of a famous parent, we then have to compete for their time and attention along with everyone else.

Famous parents are part of the family, but they are also

part of a much wider tapestry of relationships made up of the people they impact. We have to share them. Your mother, like your grandfather and all other pop culture celebrities, often struggles with balancing the pursuit of her career and craft and spending time with us, and she's right—it is tough. I know how to be your mother's balancing half, and how to be your father, because of how I was raised.

It was crucial for your uncles and me that your lola was the consistent parental presence who helped ground our family, strapping the nebulizer mask on my face at three A.M. when I had asthma attacks and cooking us food that nourished our bodies and helped us establish a connection with our mother countries. Your lola had dreams of becoming a lawyer someday—she even worked as a recruiter for the World Bank—but with Grandpa Ken's fame and three young boys in the house, she decided to leave her job to hold down the home front. And she did it with flying colors. Because someone needs to ground a family when fame is so intoxicating. I learned how to navigate the limelight of your mother's fame from growing up in my house where your lola was the grounding force. Now it is me, and your grandmothers, aunts, uncles, and cousins, who ground the family when fame takes over.

There are people who can root you, and then there are things you can do on your own to ground and balance when the winds of celebrity pick up. I learned young how to be with myself even when my father was focused on his career, away for business, and being pulled in a thousand different directions. I immersed myself in practices like meditation, journaling, fasting, and entheogenic ceremonies, not realizing that my interest in mindfulness and self-exploration would, over time, help me find my own way in life, individuated from your grandfather's success. I was also unknowingly preparing myself to be the subject of your mother's future jokes.

————

Your mother and I met at a vineyard wedding in Napa Valley, California. The day started out cloudy with a light drizzle, but as the wedding ceremony began, sunbeams cut through the parted clouds as if some sort of cosmic cooperation was in effect. I was wearing a yarmulke, a Jewish ritual head covering, and serving as an usher, helping people find their seats. I remember seeing your mother for the first time. She was wearing a dark blue dress with colorful birds printed all over. She was walking with a guy friend from high school, and I remember being instantly curious and attracted to her. I watched from afar as she and her partner walked into the rows of fruiting grapevines, clearly engrossed in their conversation, and I thought, *Why don't I ever get to meet women like that?* She approached me later that night while I was catching up with an old high school friend and invited me to one of her shows in New York, where I was also living at the time.

Fast-forward to a few months later and I am at the Gotham Comedy Club in New York City. Your mother is headlining the show and I am with a group of friends, wearing my favorite Marvin Gaye–print black T-shirt not knowing what to expect. Your mother walks onstage in a yellow T-shirt and black baggy MC Hammer pants and delivers an extremely filthy, downright hilarious set that brought on full-body shakes of laughter for me. I honestly don't remember laughing that hard before. She showed off her camel toe, pulling her black pants tight to emphasize the detail. She pulled down her pants and mooned the audience, her butt crack daring us not to laugh. This was my first live stand-up comedy experience and my first time seeing your mother perform, and I felt like I had been hit by a bulldozer of raunchy joy. I was elated and knew I wanted to get to know her better. I emailed her the next day to ask her out to lunch.

Prior to meeting your mother, I spent a year on a Fulbright scholarship researching human trafficking in the Philippines. Based in Manila, I traveled around the country interviewing survivors of sexual and domestic exploitation, hearing stories of rape, sexual violence, enslavement, and trauma. On Mother's Day, I visited a shelter for survivors filled with young women who were smiling, cracking jokes, and finding community in one another despite the trials they had endured. I was just beginning to learn the power of laughter.

My time in Manila unraveled something deep within me, blasting through long-held assumptions I formed growing up in my privileged bubble in Washington, D.C., and leaving me feeling disoriented and alienated from the world I thought I knew so well. I drove your mother crazy when we started seeing each other because I was in no rush to move things forward. After hearing the horror stories of so many women, I returned to the United States with a knowledge of sexual violence on such a deep level that when it came to dating I was hyperaware of these threads and proceeded unusually slowly and carefully. Eventually, that changed.

Your mother and I fell in love because we loved discovering the esoteric and hidden spiritual parts of ourselves, and each other, because we loved food, and because together we grew. I remember when I introduced her to her first ayahuasca ceremony in the jungle outside of Tulum, Mexico. We slept in the property owner's spacious, *Swiss Family Robinson*-style thatched hut. During the day we hiked and swam in cenotes (large, cool, freshwater open pools dotting the Yucatán Peninsula's limestone bedrock). At night we sat in ceremony in an open-air hut with mesh screens for windows, imbibing the thick, ayahuasca brew that tasted like the blood of Mother Earth and traveled deep into the rabbit hole of our minds, emotions, and beyond.

On our final night, your mother and I and a few friends left the jungle retreat to camp on a quiet, desolate beach. The mosquitoes were relentless, having penetrated the thin barrier of our worn tent, wings buzzing our ears, sharp long straw mouths aggressively poking every inch of exposed flesh. Sleep was difficult. We eventually fled the tent for the respite of the water, where we figured the mosquitoes wouldn't follow. A glowing green traced the movements of our limbs below the gentle surf. I imagined a scaly, bug-eyed eel with razor-sharp teeth had come from the deep to hunt for a late-night meal before realizing it was a luminescent algae emitting a subtle glow with each tread of the water. At one point we returned to the beach to rest and came across a nest of hatching turtles making their first voyage into the water. We watched the sun gradually peek over the horizon, and I realized in this moment that I had your mother's deepest trust. Miles away from her comfort zone, she was willing to walk with me and explore the depths of a world I had grown to love. I, in turn, would need to trust her to the utmost as I stepped deeper into her world of stand-up comedy.

I moved back to Boston in the fall of 2010 to complete my final year at Harvard Business School. Your mother visited me often, and we went on long runs along the Charles River. We made complex breakfast cereals composed of millet, steel-cut oats, and amaranth in the slow cooker I kept in my dorm room and woke to the smell of freshly cooked grains. Eventually she moved to Los Angeles for her first role on a TV pilot, a comedy on Fox starring Christian Slater. After graduating, I moved to San Francisco to pursue my tech dreams. A year and a half later, we reached a breaking point. Long distance meant we spent the majority of our time apart. We knew we loved each other, but the bigger question looming was how committed were we to each other and when would we actually live in the same city?

We were both in heavy grind mode. Your mother was acting during the day and doing comedy sets at night while renting a room at her college friend's apartment close to Pico and Crenshaw. I was working nonstop on an online business to make services like massage and acupuncture more accessible to the masses and searching for creative ways to generate income and not dip into my personal savings any more than I already had. After a year and a half of being long distance and an escalating cycle of arguments about when and where we would finally be together, I decided to take the leap and move to Los Angeles to find a place to live with your mother and discover for myself what the city had to offer. Being in a relationship will inevitably offer up uncertainty, risk, and challenges. Find someone who is willing and able to come up with creative solutions as issues arise and take leaps for you when called for.

I knew your mother was getting antsy about getting married when she started showing me pictures of engagement rings and then literally asked me when I was going to pop the question. She found a picture of an antique jade Art Deco ring that was unique and beautiful, but the jeweler told me it would chip if worn daily because jade is too soft of a stone. Despite your mother's explicit desire for the jade ring, I decided to go the more traditional diamond path, still sticking with the Art Deco style and designing all the elements with the jeweler to ensure it would look classy and unique. What I didn't know was whether your mother would love it or hate it. Once it was made, purchased, and insured I kept it in a cheap cloth jewelry pouch, the kind you get when buying a fifteen-dollar trinket on Canal Street in New York. It was less conspicuous that way if your mother happened to come across it.

I revealed the ring to her when I proposed in front of the SoHo apartment where she'd lived when we first met and where we had our first kiss. I was nervous and read a speech I'd written in my journal before bending the knee. It was a sincere and slightly awkward speech where I overused the word "pregnant" in reference to how I was filled with love for her. The best part was that not only did she say yes, but she absolutely loved the ring. Moreover, she admitted to me that she had actually changed her mind and no longer wanted the jade ring, even though she'd conveniently declined to let me know and left me to figure it out. I believe this helped further reinforce my genie-like capabilities in your mother's eyes.

On the day we got married the sun was shining in San Francisco. We got dressed together in the Airbnb we rented for the weekend in the Mission District. Then the heel of your mother's right shoe punctured her dress while she was exiting the Uber at city hall, creating a small tear. I viewed it as a sign of good fortune, like stepping in dog poo or getting pooped on by a bird. That's good luck, right?

After the short ceremony and intimate, celebratory Cantonese dinner at R & G Lounge that followed, your mother and I took a car to the Punch Line Comedy Club, where she performed, working out new material in her wedding dress because that's how dedicated your mother is to her craft. I beamed with pride from the audience, our parents and families, friends and colleagues present, as she performed her set, at one point lying on the ground with her wedding dress in the air, falling over her legs, punctured hem and all. That night, not only did we get married, but I was now the front-and-center subject of your mother's onstage material.

———

Your mother's jokes elicit laugh-so-hard-you-pee reactions. I know because people tell me this directly at the merch table after shows. Though hilarious for the audience, it requires a great deal of alignment between your mother and me to ensure her comedy is an empowering force in our relationship. Being made fun of onstage by your mother is no joke. Here is how we manage.

To start, before a performance she runs new jokes by me when I'm mentioned and gives me the right to edit or veto. I remember prior to filming *Baby Cobra* there was a joke about our sex life that I felt was a bit too on the nose. (I'm imagining you both squirming in your seats. Sometimes the truth is uncomfortable.) I asked her to modify it and she did, with a tweak to the characters. Since that day, whenever I am mentioned, she honors that I need to know in advance. And with this mutual creative trust established, I realized that I could let go. I am not here to censor your mother's artistry. I embrace her work, celebrate being a subject of it, and only ever used my executive privilege that one time. I am comfortable being in your mother's jokes thanks to my mindfulness practice, which grounds and roots me. No matter what is said onstage, I know who I am and support her in her fullest expression. But it wasn't always this easy.

It was 2011 and your mother and I were again at the

Punch Line Comedy Club in San Francisco, though this was before we were married. It was a coming-out moment for us as a couple, as I was standing between your grandparents and it was their first time attending one of your mother's shows. Your mother joked about an encounter where a man blew on her vagina as a form of failed foreplay. She talked about her body as a reggae fest that has had many guests, including a homeless man and skateboarders.

Grandpa Ken was laughing along with the audience. Your lola was generally silent followed by occasional nervous laughter. I was making the most of my peripheral vision to observe them throughout the set and take note of any perceived pleasure or discomfort. It was a meta experience to be made fun of by your mother, my then girlfriend, in front of your grandparents. Almost like stories of near-death encounters when people talk about end-of-life reviews, except this one was filled with profanity, embarrassing anecdotes, and presented in front of a public audience that responded with copious amounts of laughter. The genuine pride I felt seeing her onstage mixed with the anxiety and discomfort of being made fun of in public while sandwiched between your grandparents.

This was a big aha moment for me. Your grandparents didn't storm out of the venue, and thankfully both enjoyed the show. I found the experience cathartic, as if the laughter cleared me of ego and shame, as your mother does for so many. It was important for our relationship that your grandparents experience your mother as a performer, the same way I had years before in New York. If they could know and accept her onstage, they would then better understand her offstage, and she could be herself with my family and not feel as if she had to hide or contain herself. She did not and does not have to. No woman should. And for myself, I needed to know that my parents could handle your mother's work and in turn accept the life I was choosing. They did.

In the fall of 2018 I was the vice president of product management at GoodRx, a digital health company based in Santa Monica, and I realized I needed to stop working to support the family in new ways. Your grandpa Ken's example implied that I should be the main earner and support my family financially. But when the *Milk & Money* tour launched I knew I couldn't be a good husband, and father to you, and support your mother's career if I was also working. And because we didn't need the money, I chose to support our family by offering my time, care, and presence, forcing me to reconcile my prescribed gender roles, which wasn't always easy.

"I make a lot more money than my husband, by a long shot," your mother confidently stated in her *Hard Knock Wife* special to wild applause. She called my job an "eccentric hobby." Hearing the jokes at first made me uncomfortable and disoriented because they resonated with some truths I had to face. If I wasn't the breadwinner, what did that say about me as a man, as the son of Grandpa Ken aka Dr. Fad, as a graduate of Harvard Business School? In the challenging moments, I felt like I was failing myself, and in turn both of you.

Allowing your mother to publicly poke fun at what was a sensitive spot for me was scary at first. But over time I realized that the jokes enabled me to better see the expectations I placed on myself that didn't match our reality and therefore weren't helpful to me, or us, to continue to bear. I began to see how, similar to your lola, I provide for our family in enormous ways. I wake up and give you medicine at three A.M.

when you have a fever. I make your breakfast in the morning and know the layers of different cereals you prefer in your bowls. Therein lies the potent, challenging gift afforded to us brave, lucky few, fortunate enough to be roasted onstage night after night by your mother: that of self-realization through comedic ego destruction. Your mother showed me with her comedy how to let go of who I thought I had to be and allowed me to embrace a life rooted in my love for you girls.

Being married to a bread machine like your mother enabled me to attend your preschool concerts, Mari, have tickle fests with you, Nikki, throughout the week, and be a much more present father to you both. In addition to selling merch, I also became your mother's tour manager. My newfound freedom enabled me to work more closely with her and gave me the space to rediscover the limits of my own creative possibility, allowing me to ask the privileged question: What do I truly want to do with my one life? Now we travel around the country together from city to city, family-caravan style, your mother and I doing shows, Grandma and Lola in tow, and all of us having adventures. I wouldn't trade this for the world.

I began selling merchandise at your mother's shows when she started headlining at theaters. The first time was in Boston at the Wilbur theater on a freezing November evening in 2016. I found a local printer in Mar Vista, had some bootleg posters with the *Baby Cobra* artwork made, and manually lugged them to the airport on a red mini dolly, secured with rugged bungee cords. I manned the merch table and could tell when the show ended from the sudden roar of applause and celebratory whoops and shouts. The doors to the theater burst open and people started to stream out into the main lobby, smiles and laughter on their faces. They converged on my posters with fervor, still buzzing from the laughter, eager to talk and purchase a piece of your mother's memorabilia.

These fans were excited to see your mother perform, but more than that it was as if she was taking her audience to church like a fiery, foul-mouthed preacher who offered up profane salvation. There was the new mom who was enjoying her first night out after giving birth a month prior. There are fans who dress up like your mother, imitating the outfits she wore when you were both in her belly. There are mothers who bring their daughters. There are those who travel from across the country, and sometimes across the world. They talk about your mother being their spirit animal. Their eyes are lit up, their faces relaxed and smiling, their postures open and welcoming. Watching this magical effect on her fans keeps me manning the merch table to this day.

That Boston show was when I began to see your mother through the eyes of her fans and realized her stage presence was more than the sum of its jokes. She was speaking to people's truths and making them laugh at the ridiculousness of it all. This was what our ayahuasca ceremonies were about: sourcing the most potent parts of ourselves and letting go of the rest. Your mother, I saw, had done just that. She was embodying experiences like pregnancy and childbirth that are sacred to us as individuals, and celebrating these acts in a fresh new light. Asian cultures often teach us to be silent about our sexuality and filled with shame. Your mother breaks that up and transmutes pain and shame into power, like a mystical priestess.

Because of the way your mother viciously dissects and explores everything from gender norms to marriage and motherhood, she is like a supercharged pressure washer, removing the thick grime of long-held societal assumptions. What's important for you girls is to work with the pressure washer that is your mother's comedy to find greater personal clarity for yourselves and home in on who you are versus who you think you need to be. As both of you are increasingly characters in her comedic narrative I encourage you to set your own boundaries, and to also remember that being a subject on her stage enables people to be seen, heard, validated, and empowered. This can be a very privileged role to play. So when you do find yourself at the center of one of her jokes, ask yourself two questions. Am I comfortable with this? And, is this serving a greater good? You are always allowed to say, "Mom, this isn't okay for me," and she will always listen. Because for her, family always comes first.

During the afterparty for the premiere of her movie *Always Be My Maybe,* she had a table next to mega-celebrity Keanu Reeves. The room was teeming with actors, agents, managers, producers, and social media influencers. Daniel Dae Kim was there. Randall Park was close by. I was at your mother's table along with her closest girlfriends from college. And though these famous actors are her work colleagues and contemporaries, she just wanted to be with us, her family, her friends, the people who know, love, and ground her in all that is real. That's what you are for your mother, girls: the real.

To be brutally honest, initially I didn't want children. Living in our spacious one-bedroom apartment with your mother in Los Angeles, I enjoyed our copious amounts of free time, ability to exercise on a whim, sleep late, and binge-watch *The Wire* to our hearts' content. I clung fiercely to the independence of carefree, non-kid life. Your mother, in her wisdom, pushed for us to get pregnant, but even then it felt more like an obligation to me. Then she miscarried. And in addition to supporting your mother as best I could, I was filled with a deep, primal sadness and sense of loss. Something shifted in me that day and, from then on, I was ready to be a father, though I had no clue what it involved.

Then you two beautiful girls came into our world, Mari first, then Nikki. I remember when each of you was born, bringing you home from the hospital, the feet of your infant onesies flapping as your tiny bodies hadn't yet grown into them. I remember passing through our front door and feeling like a scared child myself, like it was somehow illegal to bring you home alone with us. Who were we to take care of you and nurture such magical beings? But then instinct kicked in, along with relatives and Sofiya, your magical Ukrainian nanny, and we were off and running on our new adventure.

Please know that you don't have to be famous. You don't have to have your own tour someday. You don't need to have a show or a movie or a book. Unless that's what you want. But you do need to be a real person with a real heart who remembers where you came from. Grandpa Ken from Kamakura, land of murasaki imo, purple sweet potato soft-serve. Lola from Capiz, land of inubaran, a stew of chicken and banana tree pith. Grandpa Wong from San Francisco, home of chizi lianggua banqiu, bitter melon and rock cod fillet. Grandma Wong from Hue, home of bún bò Huế, spicy noodle soup with pig's feet, blood squares, sliced beef, and herbs. And your mother and me from the United States, land of baggy MC Hammer pants and Marvin Gaye.

Since your birth, life has never been the same, thanks to you girls. I had no idea how much meaning and joy you would bring to my life. I often think to myself when spending time with you that "THIS is the best moment of my life," which truly happens multiple times a week, sometimes multiple times a day. And like your grandpa Ken told me long ago, all of these many random experiences fell fully and completely into place when I met you. Everything in my life, including falling in love with your mother, led me to my greatest job yet: being your father.

All my love,
Daddy

ACKNOWLEDGMENTS

My dear girls, I know we will inevitably fight and have some bad moments so I want to make sure to say this: Thank you for being onstage with me during those two stand-up specials. They truly wouldn't have been the same without you. I could feel you kicking and moving inside of me, and it made Mommy fearless because I wasn't alone up there. I'm so grateful every day for the joy you both bring to my life—a joy that I never knew could be so magical.

To my amazing husband, Justin Hakuta: Where would I be without you? Thank you for all your love and support, my darling.

Thank you to my mother, Tammy Wong, who saw *Always Be My Maybe* approximately ten times in the theater! Thank you to my father, Adolphus Wong. How I wish you could have lived to meet your beautiful grandchildren and witness everything else that has happened. Thank you Andrew, Mimi, Julia, and my incredible nieces and nephews.

Thank you to Miya Saika Chen, JEM, Sofiya Zhandova, David Smithyman, Louis Katz, Sheng Wang, Ruth Sarreal, Doug Edley, Ben Greenberg, Richard Abate, and Nahnatchka Khan.

ALI WONG is a stand-up comedian, writer, and actress. She has released two hit Netflix comedy specials—*Baby Cobra* and *Hard Knock Wife*—and wrote and starred in the Netflix original film *Always Be My Maybe*. She lives in Los Angeles with her husband and two daughters.

aliwong.com
Instagram: @aliwong
Facebook.com/aliwong
Twitter: @aliwong